Pants & Skirts

TIME-SAVING SEWING WITH A CREATIVE TOUCH

weekend sewer's guide to

Pants & Skirts

TIME-SAVING SEWING WITH A CREATIVE TOUCH

Kate Mathews

LARK BOOKS

Art Director: Dana Irwin

Photography: Richard Babb, Evan Bracken

Illustrations: Pete Adams, Lisa Mandle, Bernadette Wolf

Production: Hannes Charen, Dana Irwin

Editorial Assistance: Val Anderson, Catharine Sutherland

Library of Congress Cataloging-in-Publication Data

Mathews, Kate.

    The weekend sewer's guide to pants and skirts: time-saving sewing with a creative touch / Kate Mathews.—1st ed.

    p. cm.

    "A Lark sewing book."

    Includes index.

    ISBN 1-57990-159-x

1. Trousers. 2. Skirts. 3. Machine Sewing I. Title.

TT542. M37 1998

646.4'3704–dc21   98-4631

                                      CIP

10 9 8 7 6 5 4 3 2

Published by Lark Books

50 College St.

Asheville, NC 28801, US

For information about distribution in the U.S., Canada, the U.K., Europe, and Asia, call Lark Books at 828-253-0467.

Distributed in Australia by Capricorn Link (Australia) Pty Ltd., P.O. Box 6651, Baulkham Hills Business Centre, NSW 2153, Australia

Distributed in New Zealand by Southern Publishers Group, 22 Burleigh St., Grafton, Auckland, NZ

Printed in Hong Kong

ISBN 1-57990-159-x

ISBN 1-57990-056-9

CONTENTS

People who sew and love fabrics notice a lot in the world around them that other people seem to overlook. Patterns, colors, and textures are important elements of the world of sewing, and sewers are quick to remark on these elements wherever they appear—on stage, on the silver screen, in the throng of passersby, and even in the natural landscape. When watching a movie, they pay special attention to the costumes and visually drink up the luscious fabrics and lavish construction details. When walking through a fabric or clothing store, their hands automatically reach out and fondle the material, and their fingers instinctively pick up cues about weight, drapeability, and probable wearing comfort. In fact, it is constitutionally impossible for anybody who works with fabric to walk by bolts of cloth or garments hanging on a rack and NOT reach out and touch. When admiring a particularly dramatic sunset, sewers are most likely translating the wonderful color combinations into a specific garment or quilt design, in between moments of pure awe at nature's show.

LIFE IS A MEMORABLE PARADE OF CLOTHES

Their world, both past and present, and their own

lives are filled with the usual important dates, famous milestones, and significant personalities, but every sewer also marks a timeline with memorable clothes. It's amazing how well sewers remember exactly what they wore on particular occasions long ago. And they remember what others wore during important moments, whether fact or fiction, in real life or on the big screen. What sewer hasn't remarked on Marlene

Dietrich in a classic man's suit, Ginger Rogers in a beaded gown whose skirt swirled around Fred Astaire as they danced across the set, sophisticated Katharine Hepburn in wide-legged slacks, Tina Turner in a mini skirt, or Princess Diana in her royal bridal train?

Celebrities introduce revolutionary new styles that soon become everybody's look, from poodle skirts and micro minis to bell bottoms and men's suits. Wealthy jet setters, who traveled to resorts in Capri, Bermuda, and Jamaica, made pants and shorts the casual fashion of choice. Famous designers have always paraded skirt hemlines on the runway that seem to move up and down according to some unknown whim. The famous models in magazines demonstrate how classic fashions can come around year after year, and still look fresh and new. And sewers learn from their own successes and failures to re-craft celebrity fads into real-world wardrobes.

While it may be a long shot from the silver screen to the sewing room, personal experience with changing fashions is just as memorable. Ask any sewer about early memories and you're likely to hear about that very first sewing project, an A-line skirt with two front darts and a back zipper. You might listen to stories about classic fly-front trousers that seemed so mystifying, pleated skirts that were so difficult to press, the marvel of elastic waistbands, the fun of tiered skirt ruffles and flounces, and the sexiness of leather pants.

Sewers will also remember the garments that looked spectacular, those that fit perfectly, and the ones that never seemed to come out quite right. Then there are the embarrassing memories of popped buttons, too-short hems, and the sound of a seam ripping at a most inconvenient time—memories that inevitably advanced the skills of altering, fitting, and expert stitching. But there is no memory as warm and fulfilling as the recalled feeling of satisfaction when pattern and fabric were a perfect match and the finished garment came out even better than visualized.

YOUR PERSONAL FASHION HISTORY TEACHES VALUABLE LESSONS

Memories such as these help all sewers fashion a personal style and develop a strong set of preferences about garment fit and look. Experience teaches unforgettable lessons about what works and what doesn't, what is easy to do and what is just too complex for the amount of time available, which style is particularly flattering and which is a loser. The education learned at the sewing machine proves to be far more valuable than any "Do's and Don'ts" article, and sewers eventually learn to trust their own instincts about patterns and fabrics.

Your own sewing experience was acquired through painful trial and error, as well as triumphant success. Your sewing memories are a treasure trove of inspiration that you can turn to, when searching for the "something else" that a recently finished piece cries out for. Once you discover the pattern styles that suit your figure and work out the fitting and construction kinks, you're free to let go with your imagination and create the new stars of your own wardrobe panorama.

SEWING IN YOUR OWN REAL WORLD

But when life gets busy and your schedule is overloaded with other responsibilities, being free with your creative imagination is easier said than done. After a grueling day in the real world, the divide between celebrity fashion and your own sewing seems vast, and the challenge of coming

up with original ideas is too monumental to face. Finding the time to sew at all gets more difficult every day.

This book can help you rediscover your own unique fashion vision in two ways, by reminding you how to manage your time so you can get more sewing done and by showing you how other designers just like you have put their creative ideas to work transforming basic, quick-to-make pattern styles into memorable new looks. You will see how simple but ingenious details can be the crowning touch to a plain pattern, how a bit of experimentation can result in fresh interpretations, and how a little preplanning can help you fit sewing into your daily routine. By following a few tips for efficient planning and stitching, you'll be reenergized, motivated to sew, and inspired to create a whole new wardrobe of favorites that are destined to become special memorables.

GET READY...

With a Perfect Fit for You, and Your Lifestyle

Ask any sewer how she's doing, and she will probably respond, "I'm so busy, I can't get any sewing done. If only I had more time...." The condition everyone seems to suffer these days is being too busy. What with work, home, family, and all the other activities of daily life, you're probably very busy, too, and maybe even too busy. The four-day work week is still a futurist's dream, and it seems instead that deadlines loom larger and come around more often, requiring more work hours than ever before. The time-saving conveniences of the modern office and home were filled with promise when they first came out, but it turns out that they haven't delivered any extra spare minutes. Instead, the faxes, computers, and microwaves that speed jobs along toward completion have accelerated the pace of life, raised the expectations of what we can accomplish, and added new entries to the daily list of things that must get done. The result is that we try to cram more productivity into the same number of hours, but it feels uneasily as though we're running faster and faster on a treadmill to nowhere.

Family commitments and home maintenance chores get piled on top of work responsibilities and squeezed into already overloaded schedules, and by the time we get home there just isn't any energy (or time) left to spend on current sewing projects. Instead of being a respite from a too-busy day, the evening hours are usually reserved for even more hustle and bustle: volunteer commitments, evening classes, community meetings, exercise routines, running errands, visiting friends and family, and transporting children, not to mention the flurry of entertainment options now available, from videos to the Internet. Life is one breathless race from one date book entry to the next.

The fullness of a busy life and variety of activities can be tremendously satisfying, and we're able to achieve so much more than ever before. But the daily routine is also tremendously exhausting, and leaves little time to spend on favorite activities or personal rejuvenation. With all the other "important" things that must get done, it's difficult to justify retreating into the sewing area to dream about a beautiful skirt made out of some recently purchased wool gabardine or to sit at the machine and play around with embroidery stitches. It's a challenge to sit still and enjoy the creative stimulation that sewing provides, when there are chores to finish or phone calls to return.

FIT SEWING INTO YOUR SCHEDULE, AND GET MORE DONE!

If sewing is important to you, it needs to occupy a position of status among the various commitments of your daily life. Many of the tasks you must complete in a day are simple chores to be done; they do nothing for you in return besides give you the satisfaction of having marked them off the "To Do" list. Sewing, on the contrary, provides plenty of gratification in return for the time you spend. It stimulates your creativity, produces unique fashions that can't be found in any stores, provides some special time with yourself, and may even be a form of personal therapy by offering a way to focus your attention and rescue you from

dwelling on other problems. It's also a lot more fulfilling to work with luscious fabrics and beautiful trims than it is to wield the broom or sit through a meeting. So it certainly deserves to be among the top priorities of your life!

Why, then, is it so hard to find time to sew? You already manage to navigate a busy schedule every day without missing appointments, losing track of time, or forgetting any of the other "important" commitments. You already plan ahead to meet deadlines at work, make it to the dentist on time, and get meals done before the family starves. There's no problem arriving at the theater before the curtain rises or the movie begins. And, somehow, your hair gets cut in the nick of time and the car gets serviced before you are stranded on the roadside. But sewing usually gets pushed back to another evening, the weekend, or the next day off, whenever that may be. It doesn't have that absolute do-it-at-all-costs quality that other commitments possess. Sewing machine time just isn't the same as a medical appointment or meeting at work. Granted, you won't get sick or lose your job if you don't sew, but surely it's important enough to your personal happiness and quality of life to find time for it.

Make a date

The secret to finding more time to sew is very simple. Just make a date for it, schedule time for it, put it on the calendar. Don't make a vague promise to yourself that whenever you have some free time, you'll spend it in the sewing room. Free time will never open up before you, and if it does it will probably get claimed by something else. Just think, when was the last absolutely free day you had? Completely free of commitment and totally open to doing whatever you wanted? If, once you became an adult, you can remember **ever** having a day like that, count yourself among the very few lucky ones. For most of us, free days are an extinct species, an impossible dream, a mere fantasy. This is the real world, so stop dreaming about free time to sew, and start scheduling your sewing in a real-world manner.

Don't wait until you get home after a long day, thinking you'll set aside a half-hour after 8:00 p.m. That kind of scheduling is not specific enough or far enough in advance to prepare yourself and your energy level. By 8:00 p.m., you may be worn out and ready to call it quits

for the day. And don't assume that the upcoming weekend will provide unexpected free time. At mid-week, it may look like Saturday is totally free, uncommitted, and available to sew. But this is the real world, after all, and you know very well that Saturday won't work out that way. Something will come up, you'll notice an important event in the morning paper that you don't want to miss, and the normal Saturday chores will nag at you. At 9:00 p.m., after a long and busy day, you'll wonder where the hours went, how did you get so busy on an unscheduled day, and how are you ever going to finish that new pair of slacks?

Sit down with your calendar or day planning book, and look ahead several days or weeks. Find the logical and likely slots of time that you will be able to spend at the machine and write them down: Tuesday evenings from 7:00-8:30 p.m., Saturday mornings from 7:00-11:00

A Stitch in Time

The time you spend now altering a pattern to fit you perfectly will save you time later, because you will be able to whip up the pattern over and over, knowing it will fit right and look great every time.

a.m., Sundays after 1:00 p.m., for example. Set those precious hours or minutes aside now, and protect them as much as possible from competition with other everyday activities.

It's very likely that you won't be able to keep every appointment with your sewing machine intact, so if it makes you feel better, mark the times in pencil or erasable ink. Even if you have to use those sewing hours for other commitments, at least they made it into your schedule. And that's the point...just get it on your schedule, whatever system you use.

If you carry around an elaborate time management notebook, make the appropriate entries as far into the future as you dare. If you prefer a calendar hanging in the kitchen, pencil in your private sewing sessions. Or if your time-keeping method of choice is a changing list of things to do, make sure "Sewing" is right up there, at or very near the top. Activities and commitments naturally take on more importance when they are written down. There they are in black and white. When you made those entries, you must have had a good reason to do so. Therefore, they deserve your attention and follow-through, and you will make more of an effort to fulfill them than if they are relegated to an "if I have time" category that's dependent on your memory.

A Stitch in Time

Fitting patterns to your real-world figure is not complicated once you subdivide the process into simpler, individual steps that you can master one by one.

BREAK IT DOWN

Once sewing is enough of a priority in your life to get its own scheduling entry, it's time to get realistic about allotting time. "Sewing" is a pretty broad category to write down for a day off from work or other responsibilities. You might get so overwhelmed by all the possible sewing-related activities that you lose focus and don't accomplish much of anything. Instead, break the broad category down into component steps and schedule each one separately. You probably already use this planning technique for an office project or a big holiday party in your home.

For example, if you will have to make a presentation or submit a report at work on a certain day, you will have to plan ahead to be sure you're ready. Assuming your deadline gives you enough time to prepare at all (which isn't always the case in today's fast-paced, rush-job, now-oriented office), you will probably set aside times on the preceding days to complete certain preparatory steps. If you're having a big party at home, you'll figure out all the planning steps ahead of time: when to mail the invitations, when to plan the menu and buy the food, when to start cooking, etc. The office project and home party will both be more successful because you segmented the job into smaller, doable tasks and scheduled them individually.

You can apply the same advance planning techniques to sewing and you'll enjoy the same successful results. If you divide the broad activity of "Sewing" into smaller sub-categories, it will be much easier to find the time to complete each one. Instead of trying to schedule time to "fit pants" or "make skirt," start with more discrete tasks, such as "alter waistband pattern," or "put in zipper." When you've only got 15 minutes or an hour to sew, it will appear a lot more possible to complete the smaller steps. You won't be discouraged by how much there is to get done in such a

THE CIRCLE SKIRT
A 1950s Uniform

In the years following World War II, families moved into the new suburban housing developments started by Levittown, raised the children that became the Baby Boom, and launched rock 'n roll. Released from wartime shortages, citizens were able to buy more chrome on their automobiles and more fabric in their clothes.

In 1947, Christian Dior introduced the revolutionary "New Look," which was characterized by yards of luxurious materials in very full, nearly ankle-length skirts, cinched-in waistlines, and short fitted jackets with sloping shoulders. The New Look was designed to accentuate women's femininity and still convey a sophisticated impression.

Once designer fashions come down the runway, however, they are adapted and

THE BIG WHEEL IN A TEEN'S LIFE .. THE PERFECT CIRCLE SKIRT

transformed into everyday styles that all women can wear, and the New Look was no exception. Dior's originals eventually became the teenager's circle skirt of the 1950s. Full circles and half circles of fabric were sewn into twirling skirts worn over full petticoats and cinched in with wide belts to make the waist look tiny. Adorned with poodle appliqués and worn with saddle shoes, the circle skirt became the uniform of the era's sock hops and soda shops.

15 Things You Can Do in 15 Minutes

1. Pin on and adjust a waistband.

2. Stitch and press some darts.

3. Baste in a zipper.

4. Sew on a hook-and-eye fastener.

5. Pin up a skirt hem and try it on.

6. Cut out part of a new pattern.

7. Fuse interfacing onto several pattern pieces.

8. Clean the sewing machine and get it ready for the next project.

9. Make some belt carriers.

10. Press the crease in a new pair of pants.

11. Insert elastic into the waistband of a skirt.

12. Alter the grainline on a skirt pattern, for better drape.

13. Make a test buttonhole on your fashion fabric.

14. Do some decorative machine embroidery on a skirt yoke.

15. Arrange decorative appliqué shapes around a skirt hem and pin in place.

limited amount of time, and your sewing project will advance step by step toward completion. And that's the goal, to get new fashions completed and ready to wear.

Write it in Code

If you'd rather not publicize to the world that you've scheduled yourself to "cut pants" or "insert zipper" at 5:30 on Tuesday evening, then devise your own professional code language to describe the activities on your calendar. Designate different terms for your subcategories of sewing, such as design time, concept development, brainstorming, materials management (pretreating fabrics), acquisitions (shopping for notions), purchasing coordination (matching buttons to fabric), technical assembly (stitching time), or project management (reviewing pattern guidelines). No matter what terminology shows up on the schedule, you'll know what it means for the project you've got going in the sewing room.

An alternative method of keeping your sewing schedule private is to use a separate calendar or a daily project update sheet that can be attached to your regular day-planning system. Or apply different colored stickers for the different sewing functions you want to get done, such as red dots for planning and dreaming, green dots for stitching time, and gold stars for fabric shopping. You can also invent various acronyms for scheduled activities, such as "PSA" for "purchase supplies after work," or "S&S" to remind you about a sit-and-sew class you've signed up for. As you can see, you can get as inventive and personalized as you like with your scheduling entries. The most important thing, though, is to make sure that when you glance at your plan for the day, you will see at least one entry that helps get a garment out of the sewing room and into your ready-to-wear wardrobe.

Make a plan for the week

An efficient way to organize your sewing is to schedule garment construction according to a plan for the week. Nearly all the fashions in this book were made this way. Each one was broken down into prep steps and segmented assembly tasks that were easily completed on weekday evenings, so the designer could be sure of finishing up on the weekend. Review the "Plan for the Week" sections of each project in this book to get ideas about how you, too, can dovetail sewing into your daily routine. With the tips

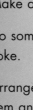

for efficient sewing in the next chapters and a plan for the week, you will be able to turn out fabulous new fashions every week of the year.

MAKE THE MOST OF THE TIME YOU HAVE

The purpose of a schedule or calendar is to make sure things get done and to keep you on track. However, every day is also filled with odd minutes and unexpected bits of time that normally flash by, but can also be put to productive use. Learn to squeeze every little snippet of time out of your daily schedule, from the minutes while your car is warming up, to the moments you're waiting in line at the grocery store or on telephone hold. You may not be able to get any actual sewing done during these short stints, but there are plenty of other sewing-related activities that will fit perfectly. For example, you can review a new pattern, compute how much fabric you need to pick up for an upcoming project, cut a few swatches of your fabric stash to carry to the shoe store for a good match, or scan a new magazine for creative inspiration. All of these brief activities make up the broad universe of sewing and contribute to your overall productivity and continuing inspiration, so fit them in whenever and wherever you can.

When you start looking for the little nooks and crannies of available time, you will be surprised at how you can find them everywhere and get good sewing mileage out of them. Get up ten minutes earlier and baste a sleeve into the armhole, pick up a lunch to go and eat it in the park while you people-watch for good fashion ideas, complete a bit of hand sewing while waiting in the doctor's office, and play around with fabric swatches from your selection while watching television, stirring the soup, or talking on the phone. When you get home, don't be distracted by junk mail or television news shows; instead, head for the sewing room for 20 minutes of decompression time and listen to the news on the radio.

You're probably already skilled at doing several things at once, so cross-train that skill to include sewing. While you're lunching out, sketch some ideas you notice in the fashions walking by. After picking up the dry cleaning, stop in for that zipper you need. When you get back home, cut out a new pattern in between loads of family laundry or fuse interfacing in place while dinner is in the

A Stitch in Time

Write down the likely slots of time in your day planning book that you'll be able to spend at the machine: 7:00-8:30 p.m. on Tuesday, 8:00-11:00 a.m. on Saturday, after 1:00 p.m. on Sunday. Try to protect those times from competition with other everyday activities.

oven. Leave for a party 30 minutes early and stop at the local sewing shop to scan the new pattern books. Once you finally get some time in the sewing room, make a buttonhole sample while waiting for the iron to heat up, put together arrangements of fabric and trim to consider while doing tedious hand sewing, or work on two garments at the same time in assembly-line fashion.

As you can see, completing two tasks at the same time can be very doable. With a little advance planning, some focused attention, and a determination to make the most of your limited time, you will get so much more sewing done. You will see that the briefest minutes can be put to profitable use, and in combination with other brief moments, will surely help you reach the finishing stages of your sewing projects. Never again will you wonder "When am I ever going to get that finished?," because you will be working on it little by little every single day.

FIT PANTS AND SKIRTS TO YOUR FIGURE, FOR BEAUTIFUL RESULTS!

A key to successful and productive sewing is to start with patterns that flatter your figure and fit you well. Why bother spending time and money on styles that don't look good

A Stitch in Time

Remember that your measurements have little to do with how clothes look and whether or not they flatter your figure.

because they are either poorly fitting or not the best choices for your unique body characteristics? Good fit takes on even greater importance when you're dealing with skirts and pants, because it involves areas of the figure that vary greatly from individual to individual and that can be radically different than the "standard" measurements of a commercial sewing pattern. The pattern companies can't possibly customize their products for the world's array of figures, so they standardize shapes and sizes for an "average" that, unfortunately, rarely matches any real person's actual measurements.

Additionally, body shapes change naturally over time because genetic heritage inevitably triumphs over strict diets and rigorous exercise regimens. Instead of forcing a changing figure uncomfortably into favorite garments from years past, it is far wiser to learn how to re-create those garments to look just as beautiful as they did before, but fit and flatter today's real-world figure. The time you spend working out the customized adjustments to ensure that a pattern fits you perfectly will save you a great deal of time later on, because you will be able whip the pattern together over and over, knowing it will fit right and look great every time.

CHOOSING STYLES THAT LOOK GREAT

There are so many different styles of skirts and pants to choose from that, with a little attention to some basic rules of figure flattery, you can stitch up a wardrobe of fashions that consistently gets compliments and admiring looks. Once you know what works best, you can stop wasting time sewing the less-than-flattering styles and concentrate on those that make you look your best. There's no better

time-saving strategy than concentrating on garments that you know will become favorites because they enhance your best features and detract from characteristics you'd prefer the world didn't notice. Over the course of your life, you have probably picked up many tips and suggestions about what works and what doesn't for particular body profiles. Dredge them up from your memory and review the following reminders before you spend any more time buying patterns, making alterations, or sewing new clothes.

General tips for flattering skirts and pants

■ Dark colors from top to bottom minimize overall weight; solid colors from top to bottom slim the figure, and minimize waistline and hips.

■ Styles without waistbands lengthen the upper body and lower the appearance of the waistline.

■ A wide belt in the same color as the pants or skirt will visually lengthen the lower half of the body.

■ To even out hippy figures, wear light colors above and dark colors below.

■ A high or extended waist can add height by lengthening the appearance of the leg; however, it also makes a short-waisted figure look even more so.

■ Bulky and pile fabrics, and too many layers, make any figure look heavier.

■ Overgarments (tunic, vest, jacket, sweater, etc.) should extend below or sit well above the widest part of the hip, to avoid accentuating this horizontal line of the figure.

■ Exaggerated details (wide pleats, big ruffles and flounces) and bold prints add weight, while small details (narrow pleats, vertical topstitching) slim the figure.

■ Gathered styles should always be made in fluid fabrics that drape well on the figure and have enough weight to hang well.

■ To flatter the overall figure, balance very different dimensions: balance wide hips with slightly padded shoulders, a large bust with pleats or gathers at the hipline.

■ Longer hem lengths can add height if the figure is already on the tall side, but will dwarf shorter figures.

■ Hems should not cut across wide points of the figure (hips, thighs, calves); raise or lower until you find the most attractive length—it's easy to see at a glance.

Tips for flattering skirts

■ Vertical lines, suggested by buttoned front openings, topstitched gores, or stitched-down pleats, slim and heighten the figure.

■ Full skirts in drapey material add height; full skirts in crisp fabric add width and the illusion of curves.

■ A short skirt makes a wide figure look wider, so choose a below-the-knee length.

■ Wide pleats can make a figure look wider, especially at the point where the stitching ends and the pleats spread apart. Therefore, stitch pleats down below the hipline if hips are wide.

■ Skirts gathered into yokes create the illusion of a flat stomach and wide hips; this skirt style is good for a figure with few curves.

■ If you like the fluid look of softly gathered full skirts but have a large waist or hips, wear a long vest or jacket unbuttoned over the skirt. The straight vertical lines down each side of the figure are slimming, but the gathered skirt suggests curves underneath.

■ A straight skirt slims all figures because it emphasizes a vertical silhouette; because the hemline is narrow from side to side, the horizontal division of the body is also narrow.

■ The wider the skirt, whether by pleats or gathers, the longer it should be, to balance the width.

■ Short-waisted and thick-waisted figures will find styles with narrow waistbands or none at all to be most flattering.

■ Short figures should stay away from hemline border prints, as they disrupt the vertical lines and shorten the figure even more.

■ Narrow pleats are flattering, because they are repeating vertical elements.

■ Pleats should lie flat against the body and not spread apart in wide areas, such as over the stomach or across the hipline. To keep pleats from spreading apart, stitch them down below the widest point or into a smooth, hip-deep yoke.

■ A full-circle skirt has too much fabric in it for most figures. For the desired swishy effect, consider other gathered styles, such as a gored skirt with godet insertions, trumpet flare style, or gathers suspended from a yoke.

■ Tiers and wide flounces accentuate the horizontal, so are best for taller, straight figures.

■ To lower the appearance of the waistline, wear a loose belt draped below the waist level or a contoured belt that dips below the waistline at the front.

■ Determine pocket type and placement to enhance the figure: don't position pockets at the hip on wide figures (see the jumpsuit design on page 112 as an alternative),

A Stitch in Time

Instead of scheduling time to "make skirt," start with more doable tasks, such as "alter waistband" or "put in zipper." When you've got limited time, it's easier to complete the smaller steps.

THE UPS AND DOWNS OF HEMLINES

Hems go to all lengths, from season to season and designer to designer, with no apparent rhyme or reason. Some say that hems go up and down with the economy, reflecting consumers' outlook on the future: up with optimism, down with pessimism. Others say hems go down as age goes up, as wearers get more conservative in their dress. Still others claim that lengths are arbitrarily chosen by designers, simply to make a noticeable change from the previous season's hemlines.

Fashion industry standards for hem length are illustrated here, and you can see the passing fads as well as the classic "keepers." For skirts, the just-above-knee, mid-knee, and just-below-knee are still considered standard for classic and professional dress. For pants, particularly dress or work styles, hems vary according to the shoes that will be worn with them.

Regardless of the fashion trends or prospects for the economy, most sewers quickly find hem lengths that are right for their preferences, lifestyles, and figures. A few quick reminders about flattering hem lengths include:

■ longer hem lengths can add height to your figure if you're already on the tall side, but long skirt lengths can dwarf short figures.

■ hemlines should not cut across any of the figure's wide points (hips, thighs, calves), so raise or lower the hem until you arrive at an attractive length. It's easy to see which is the right one!

■ pants hemmed without cuffs make legs look longer, especially if worn with matching shoes.

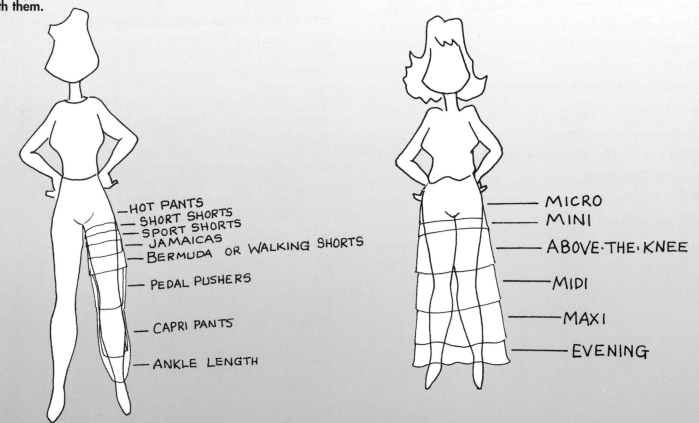

HOT PANTS
SHORT SHORTS
SPORT SHORTS
JAMAICAS
BERMUDA OR WALKING SHORTS
PEDAL PUSHERS
CAPRI PANTS
ANKLE LENGTH

MICRO
MINI
ABOVE·THE·KNEE
MIDI
MAXI
EVENING

chain inside the hem or make a facing of a coordinating fabric.

■ Straight skirts have the least fabric and so require the widest hems, to provide necessary weight. A full skirt calls for a narrow hem, because the extra fabric helps the style drape correctly and the narrow hem won't disrupt the flow or flounces of the silhouette.

■ Always let a garment hang overnight or for 24 hours before hemming, to let the fabric relax into its final shape. You may have to trim off excess fabric along the hemline that relaxed out of line. This step is essential on bias-cut garments, which may require periodic re-hemming to maintain an even line. And don't store bias garments on hangers in your closet, where they may continue to relax and stretch out of shape. Instead, fold or roll them up and stow in dresser drawers or on shelves.

■ Determine the desired length of a tapered pants style before cutting the garment out. Shorten or lengthen the pattern pieces at the indicated lines before laying them out on the fashion fabric. Otherwise, altering the hem length later can interfere with the taper of the pant legs.

■ Experiment with different hem finishes, such as top-stitched, machine blind hemmed, hand-stitched, fused, rolled, taped, serged, etc. Choose the one that best suits the fabric and its cleaning requirements.

■ Use short pieces of thread when hand stitching a hem, so the thread won't knot as much. The hem will then be held up by several lengths of thread instead of just one; if one section breaks, the others will provide back-up. You might also want to make a knot or extra-small stitch every fifth or sixth hem stitch, so the thread won't catch and pull on shoe buckles, causing a whole section of hem to draw up in gathers.

■ Press a hem lightly. It doesn't need to have a razor-sharp edge.

TIPS FOR PERFECT HEMS

■ It's more important that a standard hemline be optically even than mathematically even. In other words, the hem should look even, whether or not it actually measures the same all the way around. Depending on unique figure characteristics, such as uneven hips, uneven leg lengths, or swayback, the actual length from waistband to hem may vary a little. Don't assume that the pattern's stated hem allowance will be correct for you.

■ Ask someone to check your pinned-up hem while you stand still and move around. Once you start moving, your figure may pull the hem out of alignment. You will want to make an adjustment so the hem looks even, both at rest and in motion.

■ Mark and pin hem, and then check it with the accessories you will wear with the finished garment, such as belt, sash, shoes, or vest. The hem may have to be slightly adjusted to look straight when worn. This is especially true for pants, which may need to be lowered in back in order to cover the top of a high-heeled shoe.

■ In addition to finishing a garment, the hem adds weight so it will hang properly. Be sure the hem allowance is wide enough to provide needed weight. If you're short of fabric and end up with a narrower hem allowance, use a weight

and avoid patch pockets on the front or back side of full figures.

Tips for flattering pants

■ Pants must fit well at the hips, with enough ease to fall straight and even; to ensure good fit, buy pants patterns according to hip size and then make adjustments for waist and crotch length.

■ Tight pants emphasize all problem spots, including too few or too many curves, so choose looser styles that drape well.

■ Pants without cuffs make the legs look longer, especially if worn with matching shoes; cuffs shorten the appearance of the leg.

■ A fly-front opening adds bulk at the tummy and draws attention to this area; instead, move the zipper opening to the side or back, as in the pants shown on page 101.

■ Stirrups are meant to preserve the line of the pants, not be visible, so hide them inside low boots or scrunchy socks.

■ Rounded figures are flattered by sleek, classic trousers; cinched-in styles, such as bloomers and harem pants, emphasize the roundness.

■ Pants hemlines should **look** straight and even over the shoes; the actual hemline may be uneven, particularly if the pants are worn with high heels.

■ Move trouser pleats away from or toward center front and press them in the opposite direction, depending on what you think looks best on your figure; or eliminate them altogether and ease the pants into the waistband.

■ Cropped pants shorten short figures even more, because the observing eye doesn't see much pants length.

■ A crease in the pants leg is yet another vertical line and, therefore, is slimming. Woven fabrics hold a crease better than knits, so if you want a sharp crease in knit pants, edgestitch close to the fold.

THE CHALLENGE OF PANTS-FITTING

Many women dread sewing pants because fitting them is such a challenge. Instead, they spend hours searching the ready-to-wear racks of clothing stores for a pair that fits as well as possible, yet still looks acceptably good. However, the typical dressing-room experience is highly unsatisfying and the slacks that make it to the cash register are usually adequate, but not perfect. Most women have to settle for a too-large or too-small waist if the hips fit right, learn to live with a too-deep crotch if it's long enough to reach from front to back, or get used to shortening the leg length of every pair they buy.

If you spent just a fraction of those hours trying on ready-made pants in your sewing room or local sewing classroom instead, fitting a pants pattern to your individual figure, you would be able to enjoy the highly satisfying experience of pants that fit you well and are flattering as a result. Pants-fitting, much more than skirt-fitting, can be intimidating because there are quite a few elements that must interact correctly to guarantee comfort and good fit. Width measurements, such as waist and hip, must coordinate with other measurements, such as crotch length and depth, to achieve the correct contours for you. While this seems a bit tricky, it's not at all complicated once you subdivide the pants-fitting process into simpler, individual steps that you can master one by one.

CHOOSE A FITTING METHOD THAT FITS YOUR STYLE

There are many methods of pattern-fitting that you can consider for customizing every pair of pants you make. Consider them all and then select the one that matches your sewing style, personal preference, and the resources in your community. If you are a motivated self-learner and decide to go it alone, review the variety of books on fitting that are available at your local sewing shop, public library, or college bookstore. Because the subject is so important for every serious sewer, publishers regularly come out with new titles that introduce innovative methods, use recently developed tools and conveniences, or simplify the fitting process in a very user-friendly way. You might even find that your favorite sewing dealer maintains a lending library of videotapes on fitting, which you can follow along with, stopping and restarting the tape as necessary, and see exactly how it's done.

Many fabric shops and community colleges offer short courses in fitting and may even have quick classes on fitting specific garments. You don't have to sign up for an entire program that will train you to be an industrial pattern drafter, but you certainly can benefit from a one-day bodice-fitting seminar or three-session pants-fitting workshop. In a class, you have the advantage of an instructor giving hands-on guidance and a group of fellow sewers who need the same kind of assistance and support that you do. Besides, it's fun to work on this least-favorite part of sewing with classmates who can understand the trials, tribulations, and hilarious moments of pants-fitting.

If you're hesitant to sign up for a class, get together with a sewing friend and go through the fitting process together. It's much easier to get good results if someone can help you take measurements and evaluate the fit. You just can't take an accurate back measurement by yourself, or get a truthful all-around view of how a skirt or pair of pants hangs. Also, most women are not particularly objective about their own figures, so it's helpful to have a trusted friend identify the styles that are most flattering for you.

All of the commercial pattern companies offer basic or master fitting patterns, which are specialized garments designed for fitting rather than wearing. Each one comes with step-by-step instructions for taking measurements, assembling the fitting sample garment, and adjusting the garment to fit your measurements. Once the fit is perfected and you've got a master sample, sometimes called a sloper, you're done! Then, you simply make the same changes to any fashion pattern that you did on the master pattern. For example, if you had to raise or lower the back waistline of the fitting pattern, you will have to make the same change to that company's fashion patterns. You won't have to refit every fashion pattern you buy, because you will have already figured out the needed alteration on the fitting pattern, and you'll know in advance which alterations you'll have to make. Note that each pattern company is different and bases its sizes and silhouettes on slightly different sets of "average" measurements. Therefore, the adjustments you must make to one company's products may differ from another company's requirements.

GET TO KNOW YOUR MEASUREMENTS

The foundation of perfect fitting is knowing your actual measurements. Remember that your truthful measurements have little to do with how clothes look and whether or not they are flattering. Because of the garment styles you choose and the alterations you make to patterns, the world may never know that your waistline size or leg length does not match the so-called standard. Even if you don't make a custom sloper from a master pattern, you need to know your measurements so you can compare them to those listed on every pattern envelope. With a knowledge of your personal statistics, you can choose patterns that are more likely to fit you well and require little or no adjustment. Of course, you will want to update your measurements period-

Full waist. Take measurement following elastic or cord at natural waistline. Use the centimeter side of the measuring tape if you don't want to see the numbers in inches. Don't pull the tape too tight; accurate measurements are the key to perfect fit and wearing comfort.

Front waist. This measurement is important to know if your figure is a different size in the front than the back. Your front waist may measure more than one-half of the full waist. Take measurement from side to side along natural waistline.

Full hipline or low hipline. This measurement is taken at the fullest part of the low hip area, and is usually 9-10" (23-25.5 cm) below the natural waistline. If your low hipline is larger than the high hipline, you may need to adjust your patterns to provide extra width where it's needed.

Crotch depth. This measurement interacts with crotch length to provide wearing comfort in pants. It's easiest to measure while sitting on a flat chair or surface.

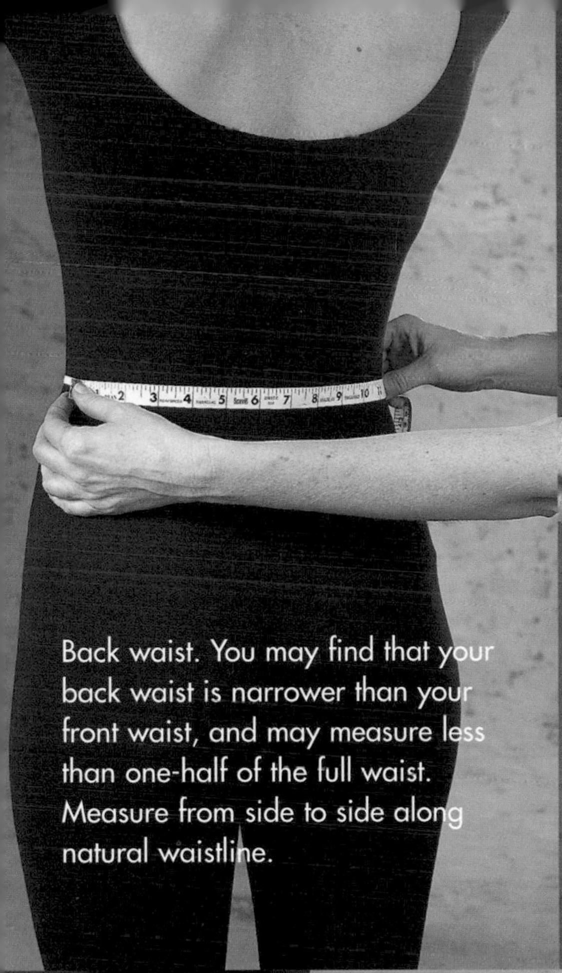

Crotch length. This measurement is important to well-fitting and comfortable pants. Take measurement from back waist around the crotch to front waist.

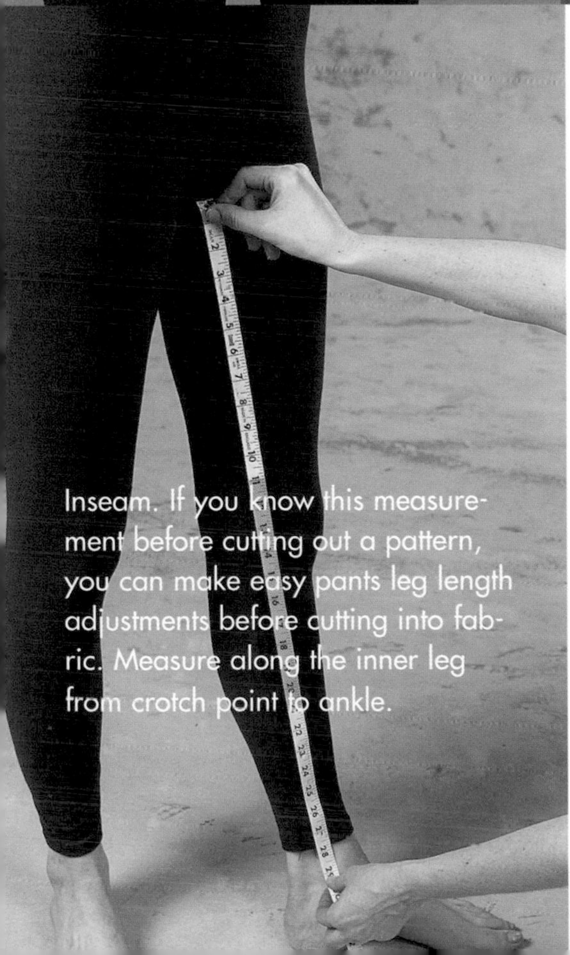

Back waist. You may find that your back waist is narrower than your front waist, and may measure less than one-half of the full waist. Measure from side to side along natural waistline.

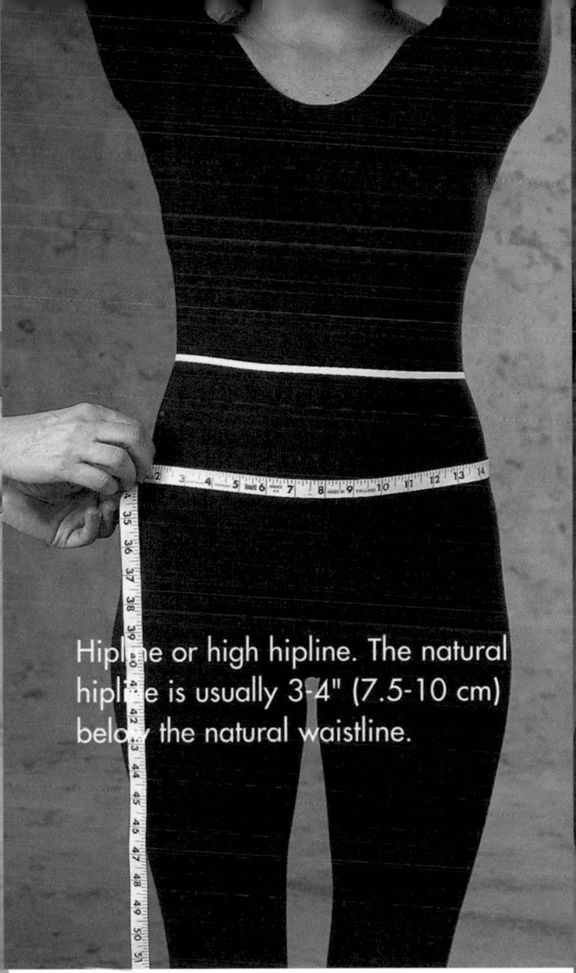

Hipline or high hipline. The natural hipline is usually 3-4" (7.5-10 cm) below the natural waistline.

Inseam. If you know this measurement before cutting out a pattern, you can make easy pants leg length adjustments before cutting into fabric. Measure along the inner leg from crotch point to ankle.

ically, to take account of any substantial changes in your figure and alert you to changes in the size or brand of patterns you buy.

To get the most accurate results, ask a trusted friend to help measure. If you'd rather not see the results in inches, use the centimeter side of the measuring tape. Dress in a leotard and tights or other smooth, snug-fitting outfit. Wrap a cord, ribbon, or elastic strip around your waist and move around until it settles at the natural waistline; then tie the cord at that level, making sure it's not so tight that it distorts the actual waist. Take a deep breath, relax, and stand naturally while your friend takes the measurements shown here. Start at the top and work down, both when taking measurements and making fitting adjustments. Record every measurement as you take it; jot it down on paper or make a chart to fill in.

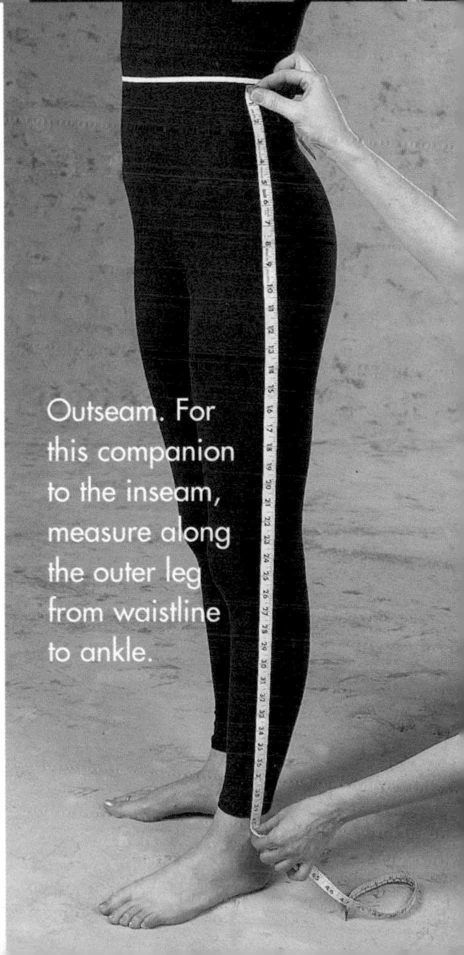

Outseam. For this companion to the inseam, measure along the outer leg from waistline to ankle.

Waist to hip. This measurement is handy to know if your hipline is higher on one side than the other. You can then make easy adjustments for an accurate fit.

Waist to hem. This measurement is important for even skirt hems. Measure both the left and right sides, especially if your figure differs from one side to the other.

Thigh circumference. Knowing this measurement will ensure that your pants legs have enough fabric to comfortably enclose the legs, without disrupting the crease or pulling at the crotch. Measure at the widest part of the thigh.

For skirts and pants, the important measurements to know are in the waist, hip, and crotch areas, and the length from waist to hem. Because your body may not be exactly symmetrical from front to back, you may want to take separate front and back measurements. This will enable you to target a specific alteration to the area that really needs it. For example, you may be broader across the front waist than the back; you can, therefore, add needed width to the front of a skirt pattern without adding excess to the back. If your figure is not symmetrical from side to side, be sure to take separate side-waist-to-hip or outseam measurements. These will be important to know when altering the garment for proper fit. The skirt on page 92 was adjusted for a figure with one hip higher than the other, and accurate waist-to-hip measurements were necessary to ensure good fit.

The crotch measurements are critical for proper pants-fitting, so take extra care with them. The crotch length is important for sitting comfort and when this measurement is off, it causes the waistband to pull down, the pants to bag in the back, or be too tight in the crotch area. When eval-uating any pants pattern, be sure that the crotch length of the back pattern piece extends further than the front, to wrap around the curve of your seat. The differences between the front and back crotch curves vary among pattern companies; experiment until you identify the brand that fits your particular contours best, so you will have less alteration to make.

The crotch depth, also called the rise, ensures that you have the right amount of garment from waist to crotch. You may need to lengthen or shorten this area, but be aware that an adjustment to crotch length may affect crotch depth. Always check one after you adjust the other.

The thigh circumference of pants should be large enough that the crease in the leg is not disrupted and the pants are comfortable to wear. The inseam and outseam measurements ensure that the pants are the right length, so you won't have to make adjustments at the hem, which can interfere with the designer's intended silhouette. Length alterations are easy to make to any pattern at the lengthen/shorten lines on the pattern sheets.

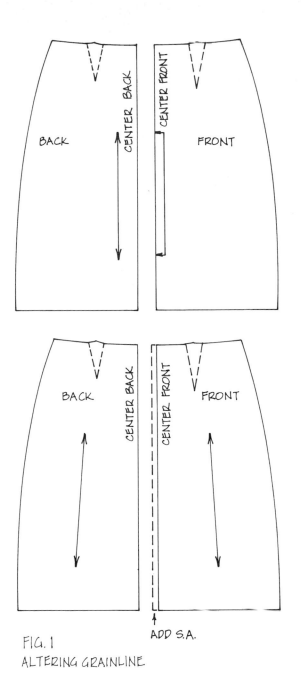

FIG. 1
ALTERING GRAINLINE

COMMON SKIRT AND PANTS FITTING CHALLENGES

The following fitting problems can be remedied in a variety of ways, depending on how much alteration is needed and your preferred method of making adjustments. Refer to a fitting book or video for specific direction, or quickly make up a muslin sample to test the fit before you cut out the fashion fabric.

Skirts hang unevenly, with too much fabric bunched at the sides

When the grainline of a skirt is parallel with the center front and the piece is laid out along the lengthwise grain for cutting, the sides of the skirt pieces end up being on the bias. The finished skirt, therefore, looks as though there's too much fabric hanging at the sides. For a flattering skirt that drapes evenly all around, move the grainline to the middle of the pattern pieces, as shown in Figure 1. Because the center front will no longer be laid out on the fold, you will have to add a seam allowance and stitch the center front seam. You may need a bit more fabric for the layout, so check the yardage before you cut, or cut the skirt out of a wider piece. The results will be worth the extra fabric.

Skirts catch or get hung up on hip and tummy curves

A skirt's wearing ease around the waist and hip areas needs to be a minimum of 2" (5 cm) and up to 3-4" (7.5-10 cm) for comfort and to keep the skirt from getting caught on the body's various curves. Alter the pattern to provide more width or choose the next larger size.

Skirts have excess fabric at the back, wrinkling just below the waist

This fitting challenge is common as figures change over the years. Most women lose a bit of height and their seat areas flatten, so they need less fabric in this area than standard patterns provide. To take up the excess, lower the waistline at center back, tapering to the original side seam, as shown in Figure 2.

Skirts or pants are tight across the front

There are several options for providing extra ease across the tummy. You can replace waist darts with soft or released pleats, or omit the darts altogether and, instead, ease the skirt to the waistband. You can add a bit of height at center front, tapering to the original side seam (Figure 3) and/or add a bit of width at the side seams, tapering to the original seamline at the hip (Figure 4). Remember to adjust the waistband length to fit.

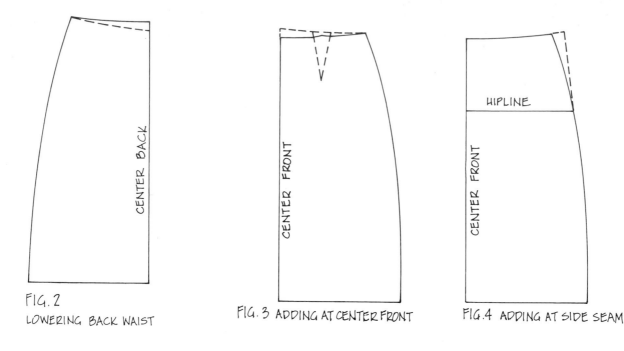

FIG. 2
LOWERING BACK WAIST

FIG. 3 ADDING AT CENTER FRONT

FIG.4 ADDING AT SIDE SEAM

The figure is thick-waisted and the skirt is tight in that area

Again, several options are available. Make the darts or pleats narrower, to loosen up the waist. Replace the pattern's fitted waistband with a fully elastic or back-only elastic waistband. Or omit the waistband altogether and make a waistline facing, using stay tape to stabilize the edge.

A wrap skirt separates when moving

This is a common problem with all garments that close in front, including skirts, jackets, and coats. The solution is simple: add extra fabric, called walking ease, at the opening edge (Figure 5) or slash the pattern and add the ease within the front piece (Figure 6). Add from 1/2" (1.25 cm) for a short skirt style to 1" (2.5 cm) for a below-the-knee style.

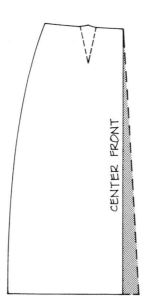

FIG. 5
ADDING WALKING EASE
AT FRONT

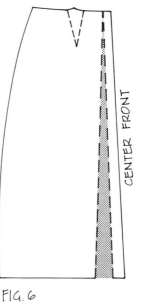

FIG. 6
ADDING WALKING EASE
WITHIN THE PATTERN

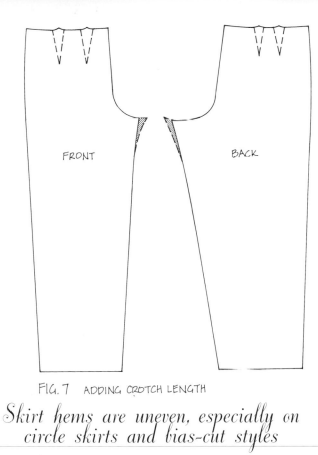

FIG. 7 ADDING CROTCH LENGTH

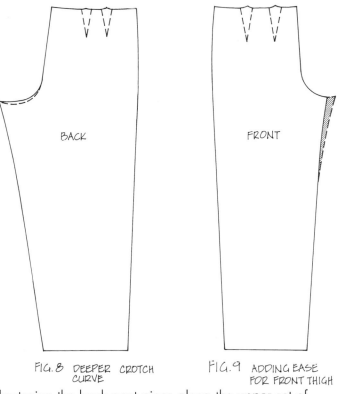

FIG. 8 DEEPER CROTCH CURVE

FIG. 9 ADDING EASE FOR FRONT THIGH

Skirt hems are uneven, especially on circle skirts and bias-cut styles

Always mark and pin up the hem while wearing the same shoes you will wear with the finished skirt. It's more important that a hem be optically even, or **look** even, than be mathematically accurate; shoes with heels can make a perfectly even hem appear crooked. On circle and bias-cut skirts, let the garment hang before hemming and use a narrow hem method.

Pants are uncomfortably tight in the crotch and ride up when sitting

The crotch length is too short, which pulls the waistband down and causes the pants to ride up. There may also be stress wrinkles in the crotch area. Add length to the front and back crotch curves by extending the crotch points, as shown in Figure 7.

Pants are baggy in the seat area

Excess fabric in the back below the seat is unflattering and disrupts the line of the pants. To eliminate the bagginess, stitch a slightly deeper crotch curve on the back, as shown in Figure 8. You can widen the inseam allowance of the back piece, tapering to the original seamline at the knee. You can also try lowering the waistline at center back or

shortening the back pant piece along the upper set of lengthen/shorten lines on the pattern.

Pants are tight through the thighs in front

This fitting challenge can be uncomfortable and cause wrinkles along the upper inseams. To increase the wearing ease, add a bit of width at the inseam of the front piece, tapering to the original cutting line at the point where the extra ease is not needed, as shown in Figure 9.

Every fitting challenge can be easily accommodated once you set your mind to it and work out the adjustments step by step. The time you spend fitting a pattern will be well worth it, because you'll know right at the outset what refinements will have to be made to any pattern. No more wasted time trying to correct the fit of a half-completed garment, and no more wasted money on fabric for clothes that are unwearable because they don't fit right.

Once you've scheduled your sewing time, settled on the pattern styles that look best on your figure, and fitted them for an accurate and flattering result, you're ready to get the creative juices flowing. You'll see how easy it is to inspire yourself with good ideas and then structure your sewing with a plan for the week, for a truly rewarding and fashionable way to spend your valuable time.

STYLE ON THE BIAS

Think of the famous starlets of motion pictures from the 1930s and they were probably wearing bias-cut dresses, softly draping swaths of shimmering fabric assembled into sumptuous and sexy styles. Bias-cut dresses were first made famous by designer Madeleine Vionnet in the early decades of this century, and nearly every fashion designer since then has used a fabric's bias to create a fluid and sensuous effect.

Bias is any diagonal direction on woven fabric, and is quite a bit stretchier than the lengthwise or crosswise grain of the fabric. The true or maximum bias is along the 45-degree angle (see illustration) and has the most elasticity and flexibility. This elastic or stretchy quality is what gives bias garments their sensuous drape. The diagonal flow of bias can be very flattering because the eye is guided in an asymmetrical direction rather than along the horizontal or vertical. However, bias garments can also cling to the figure, so a looser fit at the waist and hips is often figured in

at the cutting stage. Wider seam allowances provide extra room for fitting adjustments, which may be welcomed as the garment goes together.

The "give" of bias makes it easy to shape fabric smoothly, which is why button loops and decorative braids can be twisted, turned, and swirled on the garment's surface without distortion. It's so simple to create all kinds of interesting trims, bindings, and edgings just by cutting strips of fabric on the bias and then manipulating them as you wish.

Bias requires extra attention and care, so choose patterns with simple, uncluttered silhouettes that can take full advantage of the cut's fluidity. Garments cut on the bias use up more fabric and require additional care in handling, fitting, and finishing, so be sure to plan for extra preparation and construction time. Working on the bias can be satisfying, but exasperating, so be patient with yourself and the garment.

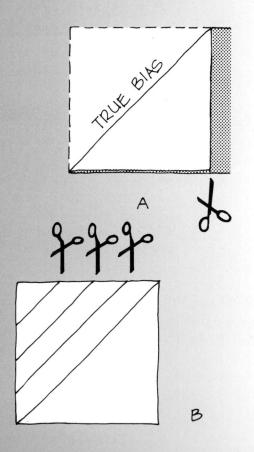

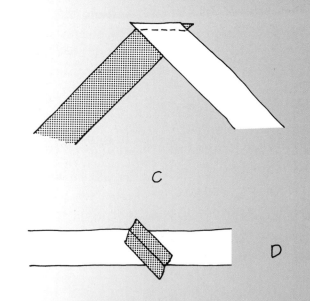

Tips for Bias Success

■ Bias-cut garments require more fabric. However, if you're short on material or don't need quite as much give, cut along any off-grain angle, particularly for binding, tubing, or edging. Even a little bit of bias will be flexible.

■ Cut fusible interfacings on the bias for flexible support and shaping. Some sewers choose not to pretreat these interfacings, because a bias cut gives them the needed elasticity.

■ When cutting out a bias garment, keep the fabric on the cutting surface and prop up the extra yardage with a side table, stool, or adjacent countertop. If the fabric drapes over the edge, it will stretch, the bias will be distorted, and the finished garment will be misshapen.

■ Use a ruler and rotary cutter to make quick work of cutting bias strips for button loops, piping, or binding trims.

■ If you're using a lightweight, swishy fabric such as crepe de chine or georgette, place the fabric on top of tissue paper and pin the two together before cutting out the pattern. When assembling the garment, you can even stitch through both layers and then tear the tissue away. Some sewers make a fabric sandwich, with layers of tissue paper on both top and bottom.

■ When basting garment pieces together, baste short stretches of the seam at a time and leave long thread tails hanging, so the seam can flex as needed.

■ Work on a flat surface as much as possible. Use a terry cloth towel on the sewing machine table to keep the bias fabric from slipping and sliding.

■ Prevent the bias edges of wrap garments from stretching and rippling by stitching twill tape or stay tape into the seam. Cut the tape to fit the paper pattern piece and ease the garment fabric to fit the tape.

■ Let bias-cut garments hang for at least one full day and up to several days before hemming, so the fabric can relax. The more drapey the fabric and closer to true bias, the more the garment will stretch.

■ Don't hang bias garments in your closet, because they may continue to stretch. Instead, store them folded or rolled in drawers or on shelves.

GET SET...

With Some Creative Inspiration

DREAM UP GREAT SEWING IDEAS EVERY DAY OF YOUR LIFE

If the idea of being "creative" is intimidating to you, you'll find that this chapter was written with you in mind. Creative skills are like any other sewing skills, such as tailoring, quilting, or machine embroidery. They are all a bit challenging when you first begin, but become easier the more you practice. Remember the very first time you put in a zipper, made a buttonhole, or pressed a pleated skirt? You were probably a little bit nervous and wondered if everything would come out all right. By now, you can probably put in a zipper with your eyes closed (or almost) and buttonholes are a breeze.

Getting your creative juices flowing is just the same. At first, your creative ideas may come in fits and starts. You may think that all your ideas are duds, losers, or dead ends. But the more you practice thinking creatively and explore different alternatives, the easier it becomes to think up neat, new ideas. Some people call this learned skill "thinking outside the box," considering every possibility regardless of how silly or unworkable it may seem at first. Pretty soon, you'll find that great ideas come to you without effort. New options will pop right

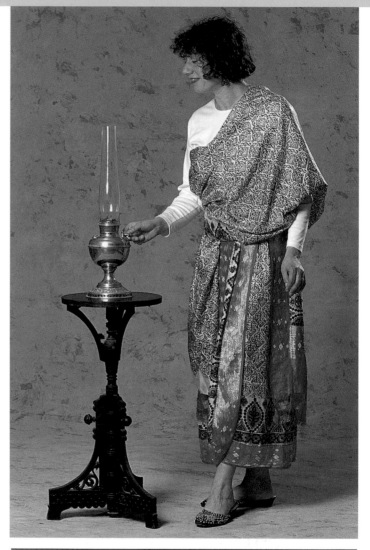

THIS EXOTIC LAYERED SKIRT BY DESIGNER LISA MANDLE IS MADE FROM TWO INDIAN SARIS THAT SHE CUT APART AND REASSEMBLED INTO A CUSTOM ORIGINAL. SHE USED THE METALLIC LENGTHWISE BORDER SECTION FROM ONE SARI, THE DECORATIVELY EMBROIDERED END SECTION THAT IS TRADITIONALLY DRAPED IN FRONT FROM THE OTHER SARI, AND THE PRINTED CENTER SECTIONS FROM BOTH. A REMAINING LENGTH OF CENTER PRINT IS DRAPED AROUND THE SHOULDERS TO COMPLETE THE LOOK.

into your mind when you're driving, sitting in the dentist's chair, or finishing up a sewing project. If you keep your eyes open and all your idea receptors turned on high, you will see things all around you every day that make you exclaim, "Wow, what a great idea! I can adapt that technique in the garment I'm working on right now."

THE WORLD IS YOUR LABORATORY OF IDEAS

Consider your surroundings and your everyday life as rich and fertile sources for creative sewing ideas. No matter where you go or what you do, you just might notice something that has creative possibilities. When you're strolling through the store or down the street, observe what other people are wearing and look for knockout new color combinations or pattern arrangements, unusual trims and details, flattering garment shapes, and interesting finishing touches. People-watching can be a most stimulating (and entertaining) activity and, if you pay attention and file away great ideas in your mind or inspiration notebook, it can also yield a wealth of raw material to fashion into your own innovative interpretations.

Watch everyone—women, men, and children, especially the teens and young adults. While most of us tend to check out what other women are wearing, it's wise to look everywhere and at everyone. Menswear can inspire ideas for fabric combinations you wouldn't otherwise think about and can even provide the components for your own original fashions, like the Peek-A-Boo pants on page 77, which incorporate recycled men's neckties. Teenagers and young adults have always put together odd and outrageous looks that often are tamed down and adopted by the famous designers. If the big-name designers can study what the kids are wearing and come up with new ideas to refashion into each season's new hits, you can do the same thing. Just keep your mind open and let the wild street fashions of your community's (or your own) kids be a starting point for your own exciting originals.

While visiting department stores or sewing shops, check out the current fashions and latest sample garments. They usually represent the most recent style trends and fabric preferences. If everything new hanging on the racks is made out of crushed velvet or denim, then you'll know what fabrics to purchase for an up-to-date, with-it look. If

you don't care what the current fashion dictates, you still might discover some stylings or details in the new velvet or denim outfits that can totally refresh your favorite "old standby" pattern styles.

While you're at the store, try some clothes on to see how the new colors or hemline lengths look on you. Experiment with different separates, to see how various components work together. Once you've modeled the season's new trouser styles and studied them in the privacy of the dressing room, you'll feel more confident making up similar styles, because you'll already know they are going to look great and coordinate well with other pieces hanging in your closet.

Scan the fashion magazines for an overview of what's "in." Even if the featured garments are a little outrageous for your down-to-earth lifestyle, they can suggest excellent approaches to stylish dressing that you can tone down for your real-world appointments. The advertisements are especially good sources of ideas for interesting accessories, creative embellishment, and perfect finishing touches. Craft and home decorating magazines can

A Stitch in Time

Costumes in movies or on stage can be gold mines of ideas for color and detail, and for ways of adapting historic or retro styles to a modern-day look.

They can be gold mines of ideas for color and detail, and for ways of adapting historic or retro styles to a modern-day look.

Don't forget the thrift shops and antique stores, where you can get up close to old or recycled clothing. A ragged 1930s velvet coat from the flea market may have a large enough area of undamaged fabric to make an exceptional vest, while an antique blouse might become the center-piece of a brand new "vintage" dress. Such recycled bar-gain fashions may be totally unusable as is, but they may provide incredible buttons, beautiful trims that aren't made anymore, or funky fabrics you just don't see today. A junk store jewel of a damaged garment may be gorgeous hanging on the wall, where its special qualities can inspire you. So don't pass up these old gems simply because they are unwearable as garments. If you keep your eyes open to all possibilities, antiquing, flea market browsing, and yard sale shopping can become profitable sewing-related activities.

Look at the photographs in this chapter to see how other designers have met the challenge of being creative. Every sewer has a distinct and individual style, and will visualize creative possibilities differently than anyone else. If you look closely at someone else's creative work, you may be inspired by a small detail or unique interpretation; it may have started somewhere else but it will end up transformed into an element of your personal fashion signature.

COLLECT YOUR EVERYDAY OBSERVATIONS

Keep records of the great ideas you notice while you're out and about in the world. Carry a little notebook or a few 3x5 cards with you so you can jot down observations or make quick sketches of what you see. The sketches are

be useful, too, for spotting fresh color arrangements and ingenious technical solutions. The color scheme of a photo spread in a home magazine can inspire your next three-piece outfit, and a crafty glue gun technique described in a recent article can simplify and speed the completion of a sequined evening jacket.

Ideas come from every-where, at all times, so keep your radar turned on even when watching television, a movie, or a theater presentation. The conservative television personalities, such as news anchors and talk show hosts, are dressed by fashion experts who stay up to date with changing trends and interpret those trends into new classics, while the more flamboyant TV stars dress up in dramatic, leading edge ensembles. If you like the way they look, you'll know how to start building a similar wardrobe for yourself. Costumes in movies or on stage, whether vin-tage or modern, are usu-ally sumptuous and gor-geous, and designed to enhance and beautify the character's appearance.

A Stitch in Time

Keep records of the great ideas you notice while you're out and about. Carry a little note-book or a few 3x5 cards, so you can jot down observations or make quick sketches for future reference.

AMELIA JENKS BLOOMER
A Fashionable Namesake

Amelia Jenks Bloomer (1818-1894) lived her entire life in upstate New York, where she also edited the Lily, a paper dedicated to women's rights. She started a "Rational Dress Campaign," which called for functional, non-restrictive women's clothing in place of the tightly laced corsets and voluminous crinolines of the mid-19th century.

This social reformer practiced what she preached. Amelia wore baggy, flowing, harem-type trousers that were gathered at the ankles. To complete the comfortable outfit, she wore her unusual pants underneath a knee-length full skirt and short jacket.

The full pants were quickly named "bloomers" and became a symbol of women's struggles for equality. Bloomers were scorned by men and most conventional women of the day, but the style was adopted by members of mid-1800s utopian communities where freedom of movement was valued and all residents enjoyed equal rights.

Amelia Bloomer was a bit ahead of her time, however, and pants were forgotten by leading edge women until the late 1800s and early 1900s, when they became active in sports, notably horseback riding and bicycling. The baggy pants that horsewomen donned to sit astride their mounts eventually became jodhpurs. For bicycling, women wore wide-legged culotte-style bloomers that passed for the day's skirt styles, yet allowed easy pedaling.

just for you, to remind you of a neat detail on a passing outfit or beautiful curved shape that would make a great appliqué. Don't depend on your memory to keep track of ideas, because life is just too busy and full of other concerns. The chances are slim that you'll remember what you observed without somehow recording, filing, or otherwise documenting it.

When you get back home, add your notes and sketches to your personal resource library. Keep file folders of ideas for garments, home decorating, trims, accessories, or other categories you choose. Tack sketches, magazine clippings, and swatches up on a bulletin board where you can see them, and where they might stimulate a good idea when you walk by. Assemble sketchbooks or scrapbooks of

ideas, or swatch files of your fabric stash in different combinations. When you're feeling dried up and uninteresting, just glance over your bulletin board or sit down with your files and scrapbooks to fire up some new thinking. Some of the ideas you saved may now seem silly, or uninspired, or unusable, but don't throw them away; just as fashion trends come and go, so will the appeal of your collected inspirations. Every time you scan your collection, it's a sure bet that something will jump out at you and suggest an idea that gets you excited—and back to your sewing machine with refreshed energy.

Let your patterns inspire you

Try to look at your stash of patterns and fabrics with a fresh eye. This may take some extra effort, especially if your stashed fabrics have been piled up for a while and you haven't bought a new pattern in months. You may be so used to making up your favorite patterns the same way that it's hard to visualize alternatives. But try to study every pattern for creative opportunities and easy-to-do enhancements. This is easier to practice with basic, simple patterns that are stripped down to their most elemental lines and free of complicated design details that cannot be changed simply. Patterns that are easy to alter or vary typically have simple lines, uncomplicated shapes, and few complex assembly details. This simplicity makes them perfect for redrawing, reshaping, narrowing, widening, or cutting apart to add decorative seams or piece together custom yardage.

While a basic skirt pattern can be a bit dull right out of the envelope, it's also a great jumping-off point for some interesting variation—and it's a quick way to get another garment completed. Simplicity is a perfect background for creative embellishment, such as manipulated fabric treatments or artful appliqué. A simple pattern also lends itself very well to creative alteration and minor adjustments to change the overall silhouette in an interesting way.

For example, start with a simple gored skirt pattern and make it up several different ways, for very distinct results. Flare the gored panels with godet insertions, as in the skirt on page 39; make the godets out of lace, sheer fabrics, contrasting colors or textures, or beaded panels. Cut the skirt gores out of alternating colors or patterns, alternate them between a horizontal and vertical stripe, or between a matte-finish solid and a sparkling metallic. Make each gore a different hem length, for an interesting geometric lower edge. Accentuate the seamlines between the gores with beadwork, decorative studs, fancy stitching, unique buttons, or novelty threads couched on top of the skirt surface; any of these techniques would create a special effect and emphasize the flattering vertical lines of the gored style as well. As you can see, the starting point of a selection of different skirts can actually be a single basic, quick-to-make pattern.

CREATE SENSATIONAL FASHIONS FROM SIMPLE STYLES

Start with basic styles and creatively vary them for a fast way to achieve sensationally unique fashions. The creative possibilities are as endless as your imagination.

■ Attach a favorite blouse pattern to your preferred pants pattern, for a custom jumpsuit. Just leave a little length below the blouse waistline, to ease into the pants waist for wearing comfort.

■ Turn any basic skirt pattern into an interesting tiered version. Trace the skirt pattern and slash the copies into horizontal panels, then add seam allowances and stitch together in graduated layers. Mix the sizes of the tiers or go for symmetry with identically sized panels. For extra stability and a smooth finish inside, stitch the tiers to a lightweight base or lining fabric and let them hang freely on the multi-layered outside.

■ Sandwich an elastic waistband between two lightweight skirts for a quick and easy reversible fashion.

■ Experiment with the interplay of layered skirt fabrics, such as white eyelet over a dark-colored underskirt.

■ Have fun with different pants hem options, such as a reverse facing band, Ultrasuede cut-out appliqué, self-fabric drawstring through buttonholes around the hem, a wraparound strap that laces up to mid-calf, decorative embroidery or cutwork, or a pegged hem with an ankle slit.

■ Vary the side seams of any skirt for interest. Create a side opening with button placket, button loops, or a lacing. Leave a long unstitched slit, and add a contrast panel underneath the seam. Add godets for side seam flare or a graphic zigzag of metallic braid. Random placement of beads, studs, unusual buttons, or other fun trims can turn any skirt into a creative fashion landscape.

■ Vary the hem of a basic skirt with trumpet flare shapes, flounces, ruffled underskirt, or shaped hem like the tulip skirt.

BLUE JEANS
An American Legacy

Blue jeans, denims, jeans, dungarees, Levi's. Whatever you call them, this basic American garment has got to be the longest-lived fashion trend in history, and it shows no signs of fading into memory.

Back in 1850, at the height of the Gold Rush, a recent immigrant named Levi Strauss joined the legions of hopeful men who traveled to California in search of fortune. Strauss did find his fortune, but not in the gold nuggets panned out of streambeds or picked out of the mines that tunneled deep inside the mountains.

Seeing the miners' need for rugged work clothes, he fashioned some brown canvas that had been originally planned for tents into durable pants. After putting them to the test in the gold mines, Strauss improved his early designs by adding double stitching for extra strength and the now trademark copper rivets at stress points, to keep the pockets and seams from tearing.

As demand for his work clothes grew, Strauss switched from the canvas cloth to a durable cotton yardage from Nîmes, France. The cloth from Nîmes (or de Nîmes) was quickly Americanized to "denim." When he began dyeing the cloth with indigo, denim then became synonymous with the color blue.

Jeans remained the preferred dress code for hard-working generations of Americans, from cowboys to carpenters, farmers to railroad men. They also became the symbol of various social outcasts in recent American history, including the motorcyclists of the 1950s movie, *The Wild One*, and the hippies of the 1960s music festival, Woodstock.

But this is a democratic country, and denims were destined to be appropriated by all. Ever ready to adapt a good idea when they see one, the big-name designers, such as Dior, Calvin Klein, and Gloria Vanderbilt, tamed the outlaw image of denim jeans and turned them into the fashion must-haves of the 1970s. The Gold Rush miners of the 1850s would never have believed that the label on the back of their jeans might someday be worth more than their daily gold harvest.

From the mines of history to the mainstream department stores of today, blue jeans are the signature American garment—durable, casual, comfortable, and recognizable around the world.

Basic as they are, skirts can be jazzed up in many ways. Possibilities for creative interpretation are limited only by the imagination. A flared skirt can look even more romantic with a hem that dips and undulates. A straight skirt can take on multiple identities with added drapes and overlays, snap-on or button-on tiers, or detachable aprons. A wrap skirt can overlap in the front or back, or even at each side seam. A full skirt can be varied with a shaped or asymmetrical hemline, or a hem ruffle that attractively peeks out at the bottom. Hems can be dressed up with all manner of fringes, trims, braids, or border prints. Pleated skirts take on assorted personalities depending on whether the pleats are unpressed, sharply creased, or stitched down in different patterns; a decorative stitch motif at the top of a kick pleat or the point where pleats release can

A Stitch in Time

When working with custom-pieced yardage, choose patterns that are simple to construct, so you can focus on the fabric's design rather than the assembly.

be a unique design exclamation point. Reversible styles provide double the design mileage for the single construction effort. Make a simple skirt in two layers of fabric and create subtle, artistic effects with pastel sheers or eyelet materials over richly colored solids, like a painter layers pigments on the canvas. Use your inspiration resource library to help you devise even more ways to turn the simplest of styles into the most innovative of fashions.

Simple pants patterns can be similarly altered and varied. Palazzo pants can be made out of sheer fabric or cut-out eyelet, and then worn over solid-colored leggings. Wide-leg pants hems can be cinched in with drawstrings or elastic, or embellished with appliqué designs. Side seams can be decorated with non-functional buttons, swirling designs of ribbon or braid, piping, or simple topstitching. Ingeniously shaped patch pockets can be surprising and

A Stitch in Time

Combine decorative stitches on your sewing machine to make totally new motifs. Even a zigzag stitch can look interesting in a decorative thread and in combination with another stitch.

creative touches, and placed in ways that camouflage figure challenges, such as in the jumpsuit on page 112. Culottes and walking shorts can be widened and lengthened, to create comfortable skirt-like garments. Add a geometric appliqué of Ultrasuede or braid to a crisp fabric for a gaucho look, or cut from a swishy sheer for a sensuous and fluid look. Have fun making different shaped belt carriers (see page 55) or detachable sashes that add drama and disguise undesirable figure profiles.

Don't forget that patterns don't have to stand alone or go together exactly as the manufacturer intended. You can mix and match pattern components just as you do the various separates in your wardrobe. Many designers in this book take favorite elements from one pattern and incorporate them into other styles they make, from a forgiving waistband to convenient pockets. Even if you don't know anything about pattern drafting, combining pattern parts is an easy way to customize your fashions, according to your preferred fit and tastes.

TAKE ADVANTAGE OF THE FABRIC'S SPECIAL QUALITIES

When you are assessing your favorite patterns for new creative possibilities, get out swatches of your fabric inventory and set them out where you can see them. You might see

A Stitch in Time

Patterns and fabrics work together to create fashion, so keep your mind open to new and unusual partnerships.

some exciting new combinations you hadn't noticed before. The stripes of a particular fabric might be perfect for a certain pleated skirt pattern, resulting in a flashy change of color as the skirt pleats move. The subtle floral print of another fabric might lend itself to some delicate beaded embellishment on the yoke of a skirt or along the hemline of some dressy pants. Just a small touch can create a memorable look, such as a wild red silk piping down the side seam of black evening pants, or a meandering trail of sequins around the bottom of a skirt flounce. Patterns and fabrics work together to create fashion, so keep your mind open to new partnerships.

Carry the fabrics that are awaiting marriage with the perfect pattern into your bedroom or dressing area and arrange them with other garments in your closet. Look for interesting new combinations or for features on clothes you have already made that would work well for the unsewn yardage. Hang swatches or lengths of fabric in or near your closet so you can be thinking of possibilities while you dress. Carry swatches with you at all times, or hang them up in the kitchen, office, or from the rearview mirror in your car. People may think you're a famous fashion designer, or just plain weird, but you will be unconsciously thinking about those swatches all the time. Then, you'll be ready to latch onto a great idea that strikes at unpredictable moments. When your fabrics are stored away, out of sight, they won't spark creative ideas as they will when they are visible.

Put yourself in creative environments

You can often stimulate your creativity by putting yourself in situations that get the mind thinking in new ways. A sewing class or lecture may awaken you to new techniques or trends you didn't know about. And it's not unusual to walk out at the end of an interesting presentation feeling fired up, inspired, and motivated to go home and sew all night. Networking with sewing friends often gets the

Completed garments can often inspire creative ideas for companion fashions. Designer Lisa Mandle uses some pretty buttons and a meandering decorative appliqué treatment around this skirt hem to create an equally interesting partner for this delicious blouse.

advances in sewing technology. A stroll through a local art or crafts gallery, or a simple walk in the woods, can also do a great job of inspiring new ideas or reenergizing you.

When you're overflowing with creative ideas and you're ready to sew, you don't want to be hampered by inefficiency or lack of organization. Now that the hard part is over—selecting flattering styles, fitting them to your individual figure, and dreaming up great ideas for special treatments—the actual preparation and construction procedures should be as streamlined as possible, to get your visions of unique fashions from conception to reality as quickly as possible.

THE USE OF TRIANGULAR INSERTIONS, OR GODETS, IN CONTRASTING FAB-RIC ADDS FLAIR TO A GORED SKIRT AND COORDINATES NICELY WITH THE MAIN SKIRT FABRIC FOR AN INTERESTING RESULT. HERE, A TAILORED NAVY BLUE LOOK IS VERY DIFFERENT THAN THE FEMININE WHITE SILK AND LACE.

creative juices flowing, as ideas are exchanged along with stories about stitching disasters and successes. Attending a regional sewing, quilting, or fashion industry show will provide lots of stimulation and alert you to new and helpful

EACH COMPONENT OF THIS MULTI-PIECE ENSEMBLE BY DESIGNER SHEILA BENNITT INTERRELATES WITH THE OTHERS, MAKING THE FINISHED COLLECTION A VER-SATILE WARDROBE FOR TRAVEL OR DAY-TO-EVENING WEAR. A SWITCH FROM LONG SKIRT TO SHORT SKIRT OR PANTS, ALONG WITH CHANGING ACCESSORIES, HELPS THE WEARER GET MAXIMUM MILEAGE OUT OF FOUR EASY CORE PIECES.

THIS WIDE LEGGED CULOTTES STYLE BY DESIGNER SHEILA
BENNITT IS SO COMFORTABLE AND CAN BE WORN IN TWO
VERY DIFFERENT WAYS—DRESSED UP IN A SKIRT AND HIGH
HEELS, OR FUN AND FUNKY WITH THE LEGS TUCKED INTO HIGH
BOOTS.

THE COTTON KNIT COMPONENTS OF THIS
ENSEMBLE BY SEILA BENNITT ARE BUILDING
BLOCKS FOR SEVERAL DIFFERENT LOOKS.

Designer Sheila Bennitt made this glittering outfit to wear at Carnival in Rio de Janeiro. To maximize comfort in the crowds and heat, she used silk netting and other sheer fabrics for the loose balloon pants, tank top, and lacy wrap. The glitter and sequins meant she could leave her good jewelry safely at home.

THESE PANTS BY DESIGNER LISA
MANDLE ARE PLEATED IN THE FRONT
AND ELASTICIZED IN THE BACK, FOR
THE GREATEST WEARING COMFORT.
SHE CUT THE SIDE FRONTS OUT OF
BLACK FABRIC TO CONTRAST WITH
THE INSET POCKET AND PROVIDE AN
UNEXPECTED TOUCH THAT ALSO SLIMS
THE WAISTLINE. SUCH SIMPLE TOUCH-
ES CAN MAKE ANY BASIC FASHION
STAND OUT FROM THE CROWD.

Designer Lisa Mandle treats the hem area of her skirts as creative opportunities for artful embellishment. Beautiful trim and fabric manipulation at the center back hem will guarantee admiring glances when the wearer exits a room.

It's easy to customize trendy patterns and garments to match your real-world lifestyle. Mock wrap skirts are all the rage now, but can inconveniently blow open on a windy day or part ways a little too easily when you walk. Designer Sally Hickerson makes the most out of a contemporary style without sacrificing wearing confidence, by altering the pattern to achieve a more generous overlap and underlap.

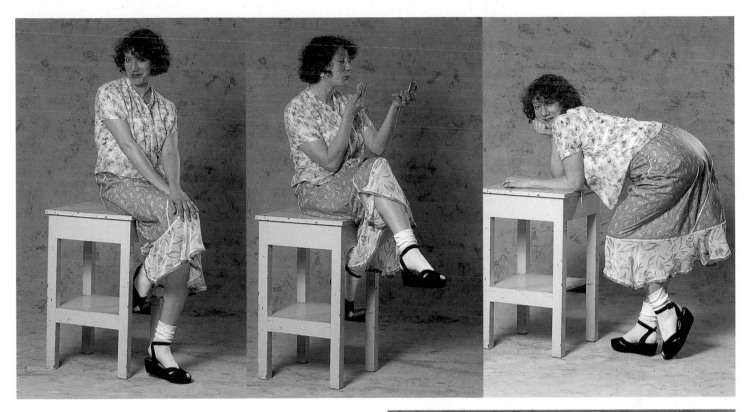

ABOVE, DESIGNER LISA MANDLE ADDS A SHEER CHIFFON FLOUNCE, EDGED HEM, AND MEANDERING DECORATIVE CORDING TO A BIAS-CUT SKIRT. AT RIGHT, SHE USES MULTIPLE LAYERS FOR INTEREST.

GET READY...
GET SET...
SEW

STREAMLINE SEWING FOR OPTIMUM EFFICIENCY.

You have worked hard to maximize the available time in your busy schedule, customize your favorite pattern styles to fit and flatter your figure, and rejuvenate your private stock of creative ideas. Now, the challenge is to follow through with the same energy and sense of purpose during the sewing steps and all the way to the finishing stages of your fashion creation. This is not difficult to do. Simply take the same organized approach to your sewing that you did to your schedule-planning, pattern-fitting, and idea-collecting.

If you break down the preparation, stitching, and finishing processes into discrete, manageable tasks, you'll discover that it is easier to find time to sew during a typically busy week. And if you take advantage of various tricks and tips for efficient sewing, organizing supplies, and using equipment that speeds up the work, your garments-in-progress will reach their final stages almost without effort. With a little preplanning and ingenious thinking, you can seamlessly dovetail the preparation, stitching, and finishing stages into your everyday schedule, and get new clothes into your closet rather than seeing them detoured in your sewing room. You'll also keep yourself charged up about sewing if you can whisk projects out the door instead of letting them languish in various stages of completion.

When you're excited about starting on a new project, it's tempting to leave the previous one behind, waiting for hem, buttonholes, decorative trim, or that special "something else" you haven't quite thought up yet. Sometimes, you need to be patient with this "almost-finished" state so your creative mind can subconsciously work on coming up with the perfect final touch. However, if you consistently end up with a bunch of unfinished garments because you're so busy working on new ones, it will pay to organize your schedule, your ideas, your sewing area, and your stitching habits to help you finish what you start.

SELECTING PATTERNS FOR EFFICIENT SEWING

A key to streamlining the sewing process is to start with patterns that are chosen for efficiency. Look for simple, uncomplicated, unstructured patterns that can be put together quickly. Study the line drawings for each pattern, rather than the photographs, to determine the general construction of the garment. You can see the garment's style lines more clearly in the drawings than the photos, which are composed to give you an overall profile but may not show important details. A style that has few components, straight seams, and a simple overall silhouette will be far simpler and speedier to assemble than one with many different jigsaw-puzzle-like pieces, curved or asymmetrical seams, and a complex shape. For example, a simple A-line skirt with a few waist darts will be a less challenging or time-consuming project than a knife-pleated style or many-gored skirt with shaped seam insertions, and pull-on pants with an elasticized waistband will go together faster than classic cuffed fly-front trousers.

A Stitch in Time

If you're working with many different colors in the same piece, use gray thread, which tends to blend with most fabric colors. You'll save time because you won't be changing thread every few minutes.

The pattern companies conveniently offer guidelines that help you determine a pattern's simplicity and ease of assembly. Labels such as "Easy," "Make it in an hour," "Knits only," "Designer," and "Advanced" are helpful aids for identifying patterns that will be good choices for both your tight schedule and the specific fabric that's waiting at home. Some sewers use these identifying terms as useful starting points for pattern selection, while others ignore them totally and go by their own experienced judgment, based on the drawings, photographs, and descriptions on the pattern envelope. Beginners are usually advised to stay away from "Advanced" or "Designer" patterns and instead purchase the "Easy" versions, so they can learn the basics of sewing construction and not be discouraged by complicated tailoring or excessive detailing. However, your own sewing experience may lead you to believe that "Easy" patterns are too brief in their instructions or leave out construction details that you feel are essential to a quality garment. You may find that "Designer" or "Advanced" patterns are actually easier to use, because they are more detailed and therefore go together in a very logical step-by-step process. Again, study the drawings and read the description on the pattern envelope to help you choose styles that are right for your available sewing time and level of skill.

It's worth repeating (over and over) that you should reuse the patterns you've already tested and altered to fit your figure correctly. Once you've worked out the kinks and you know these styles look great, use the patterns over and over, varying them each time to create different versions of a flattering garment. Most observers will never notice that the skirt you're wearing today is actually the same one you wore yesterday, underneath the interesting detailing or unusual pieced fabric treatment. Instead, they will probably notice that you have an amazingly attractive and varied wardrobe, and the ensemble you wear on any one day will be fresh, new, and uniquely yours. Why tell them that you work with just one or a few patterns, that most of the skirts you wear actually come out of the same pattern envelope? Let the world be dazzled by the creative design and interesting variety of your wardrobe; only you will know how basic the underlying construction is.

While working with old-standby styles is a sure bet for efficiency and productivity, it can be immensely profitable to try out new patterns when you've got time to do so. There are many exciting new pattern companies in the sewing industry these days, turning out wonderful new garment designs every season. Try to work some "laboratory time" into your sewing schedule, when you can experiment with these new designs. Stitch them up quickly in muslin, or try them out with some fabric that's been waiting to be turned into three-dimensional form. You just might discover a brand new, perfectly fitting (or easily altered), gorgeous style that will become your newest dependable, tried-and-true pattern.

However, leave the experiments for the days when you've got extra time or when you're not on a deadline, trying to make a new pair of slacks for an important Monday meeting. Doing anything new on a tight deadline, sewing included, increases the risk of error and frustration. You probably wouldn't choose to cook a previously untested recipe for an important dinner gathering at your home; instead, you'd try it out on family or friends beforehand, so problems can be identified during the trial run and adjustments can be made for a problem-free success later on. By the same token, don't labor over a new pattern style, hoping it will come out right for a must-look-good occasion. Try it out ahead of time, work out the fitting kinks, reorganize the construction process to suit your personal sewing habits, and get comfortable with the finished look. Then, when you make up the pretested pattern, you'll know what to expect and will be able to breeze through construction with confidence that the results will be perfect.

Work your "sewing lab time" into your regular schedule. For example, spend a few minutes studying the instruction sheets while waiting for the iron to warm up, a half-hour to pin-fit the tissue pattern pieces while doing laundry, or fifteen minutes to evaluate the pattern for creative variation before heading out for the day. Use the odd moments and brief fragments of time to explore new pattern possibilities, step by step, and you'll continue to broaden your inventory of "old-standby" patterns. You can also take a week or two off from your regular sewing schedule and designate those evenings and weekend days as your "research and development" time, when you test out several new patterns you've collected. Regular experimentation with new styles and techniques, even when squeezed bit by bit into an already-overbooked schedule, is crucial! It will keep you refreshed, creatively stimulated, and motivated to continue sewing.

SIMPLE DOESN'T HAVE TO MEAN BORING

When your goal is to get more sewing done in the midst of a dizzying array of competing responsibilities, you'll be more successful if you start simply. While a simple pattern may seem boring or undistinguished at first, at least you will know that it won't require too much time to make, and you can later draw on your stores of good ideas to transform the basic look into a dynamite custom fashion. Basic styles, with their simple shapes and uncomplicated lines, are great starting points for creativity. An easy straight skirt can be an empty canvas that you dress up with unusual appliqué shapes, swirls of decorative braid, or sparkling beadwork. Simple pull-on pants can look much more interesting with inventive side seam treatments, appealing draped sashes, or fresh and fun cutwork patterns. When you start with a simple construction process, the basic garment goes together in a flash. Then you can enjoy the "fun" time, when you dream up distinctively creative ways to transform simple into sensational. Don't get bogged down in complicated assembly steps; instead, get the basic sewing over with as quickly as possible, so you can keep yourself jazzed up and energized with the creative problem-solving stages of fashion design.

You can also mix and match your oft-used simple patterns, combining elements from one with interesting features from another to create new variations or to further streamline your stitching. For example, pull a quick-and-easy pocket from one pattern and use it in place of the more complicated version on your favorite pleated pants pattern. Swap the waistbands between two skirt patterns, for faster construction or greater wearing comfort. Or adapt the decorative seam-finishing technique from a trouser pattern to the skirt you're making, for a different look.

SELECTING AND PREPARING FABRICS FOR EFFICIENT SEWING

Even though fabric shopping is an affair of the heart rather than the head, it's wise to think about easy care, easy wear, and easy-to-work-with fabrics before spending your hard-earned money. This does not necessarily mean you should buy only those old-fashioned "wash and wear" synthetics. They may be great in the washing machine, but are usually uncomfortable to wear, tricky to sew, and never hang quite right. There's a brave new world of fabrics out there these days, which makes fabric shopping a particular pleasure. And the varied fabric care requirements make it easier to find materials that are right for your lifestyle, schedule, and the patterns in your To-Do lineup. All fabrics differ from one another in the way they sew, drape, and wear. But depending on your lifestyle and preferences, you can quickly narrow the wide selection down to a workable core of desirables.

First, look for fabrics that are good matches for your patterns. For example, if your next garment will be a bias-cut swishy skirt, don't choose a stiff oxford cotton; it just won't hang correctly and certainly will never swish against your legs. Instead, go for a drapey rayon or silk to be sure the fabric and pattern style are well-matched and will provide the desired effect. On the other hand, a crisply tailored pair of classic trousers just won't work right if you make them in silk chiffon or other fluid fabric, because those

A Stitch in Time

Press the creases in classic trousers before stitching the crotch seam, aligning the crease with the pleat closest to center front. It's easier to lay each leg flat on the ironing surface when it's not attached.

materials won't provide the structured, crisp look you're after. Feel free to experiment by pairing pattern styles with seemingly incompatible cloth, because you may discover some interesting and unusual effects that you wouldn't have thought about. But if you're strapped for time and need to get some slacks or a skirt made up fast, stick with combinations of fabric and style that you know will work.

In addition to compatibility with pattern styles, you should prefer fabrics that will go easy on your dry-cleaning budget and wash-day schedule. Your goal is to turn out fashionable garments in an efficient and time-saving manner. However, if everything you make spends too-frequent intervals at the dry cleaners and costs you dearly, you may feel that sewing is an expensive habit that keeps your local cleaning establishments in business. If you want your clothes in the closet, available to wear as much as possible, look for fabrics that you can tend yourself. You will be able to find washable fabrics more readily than ever

"PRESHRINK YOUR FABRICS!"

FORGIVING WAISTBANDS

As we age, we tend to kiss our tiny waistlines goodbye, that is, if we ever had them to begin with. And with each passing year, we tend to get more and more impatient with tight and uncomfortable garments, especially in the waist area. Our waists seem to expand and contract unpredictably, despite our dedicated exercise programs, and we're always fighting the battle to fit clothes for the long term. If your waistline seems to fluctuate by the hour, day, or month, here are two of designer Mary Parker's methods of elasticizing skirt waistbands quickly and easily, without adding extra bulk.

Front

Back

Elasticized back waistband

This version uses regular elastic in the back only and leaves the front unchanged.

1.

Measure the upper edge of the garment back between the side seamlines. Do not fold out any darts or pleats before measuring, because you will not be sewing them in this version. NOTE: You can measure the upper edge of the back pattern piece and multiply by two, to get the full back measurement; do not include seam allowances.

2.

Measure garment waistband pattern piece from the side seam to center front.

3.

Add these two measurements together and multiply by two. The result should be at least 2" (5 cm) larger than your actual waist measurement.

4.

Add appropriate seam allowances for the closure method used by the pattern. For example, a zipper closure will require two standard seam allowances, but a pocket placket type opening will require one standard seam allowance plus the length of the entire pocket top.

5.

Make a new waistband pattern of the above length and

3¾" (9.5 cm) wide. This will result in a finished width of 1¼" (3 cm).

6.

Mark the portion of the waistband that will be attached to the front of the garment. Interface this portion as you normally would. Also mark and interface any area of the waistband that will be attached to the top of a pocket. Do not interface the rest of the waistband.

7.

Construct the garment up to the waistband attachment step, omitting any back darts or pleats. Press waistband in half lengthwise. Press under the seam allowance on one long edge and trim.

8.

Sew the top edge of the garment to the unpressed waistband edge, pleating, gathering, or easing the garment front to fit. The back will not need gathering or easing because the back waistband was cut to equal the garment back measurement.

9.

Turn the waistband to the inside and overlap the pressed-under edge of the back waistband over the previous stitching. On the right side, stitch in the ditch of the previous seam, being sure to catch the folded-under waistband edge. You will stitch the front portions of the waistband after inserting the back elastic.

10.

Measure the original waistband pattern between center back and a side seam; multiply by two. Add 1" (2.5 cm) to this measurement and cut this length of elastic.

11.

Insert elastic into the casing made in step #9 above. Secure elastic at both side seams by pulling it ¾" (2 cm) beyond the side seam and stitching across it, through all layers.

12.

Stitch each end of the waistband, right sides together. Trim, turn, and press.

13.

Overlap the pressed edge over the previous seam and stitch in the ditch, as you did on the back waistband in step #9 above.

All-over stretch waistband

This version uses a Ban-Roll type of elastic in both the front and back, giving just the right amount of stretch to a tailored waistband.

1.

Fold out any darts or pleats on the front and back pattern pieces and tape in place temporarily.

2.

Measure the upper edges of the garment between the side seam allowances. The result should be at least 2" (5 cm) larger than your actual waist measurement. NOTE: You can measure the upper edges of the front and back pattern pieces and multiply by two, to get the full front and back measurements; do not include seam allowances.

3.

Add the measurement of any extensions and seam allowances shown on the original waistband pattern. Cut your waistband to this length and 3¾" (9.5 cm) wide.

4.

Cut a piece of elastic 2" (5 cm) shorter than the measurement in step #3.

5.

Construct the garment as usual up to the waistband attachment step. Do not interface the waistband.

6.

Mark seam allowance and extension on the ends of the

elastic. Divide and mark the remaining length into four equal sections. If your front waist measurement is greater than your

back waist measurement, move the side marks a little toward the back, so that the front waist is slightly favored.

7.

Press the waistband in half lengthwise. Press under the seam allowance on one long edge and trim.

8.

Sew waistband to the skirt. Pin the elastic to the seam allowance, distributing it evenly over the front and back.

9.

Sew the elastic to the waistband/skirt seam allowance with a zigzag stitch, stretching it slightly to fit the edge of the skirt. Do not stretch the elastic in the seam allowances or extension at the ends of the waistband.

10.

With right sides together, stitch each end of the waistband, catching the elastic. Trim corners and turn right side out.

11.

Turn the pressed-under edge of the waistband to the inside, overlapping it slightly over the previous seam, and stitch in the ditch, stretching the elastic slightly as you go.

PLEAT PRIMER

Pleating is a basic method of shaping or manipulating fabric to control fullness where desired, as in a skirt, the back of a shirt, or the waistline of trousers. It can also be used decoratively, when the pleats are stitched down in different arrangements to form interesting patterns.

Accordion

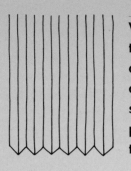

Very narrow pleats, narrower at the top than the bottom so they fan out at the bottom of the pleated area and form a zigzag edge. Also called sunray and fan pleats. Accordion-pleated fabric is often available by the yard for quickly making skirts.

Box and Inverted

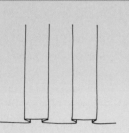

Box. Formed from two pleats facing in opposite directions.
Inverted. Formed from two pleats that face each other and meet along the center of the pleat. A kick pleat is a short inverted pleat at the bottom of a narrow skirt, to provide extra room for movement.

Cartridge

Small tubular pleats inspired by loops for bullets on military cartridge belts; they are normally not pressed flat.

Cluster

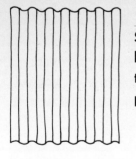

Narrow pleats arranged in groups instead of distributed evenly across the fabric.

Knife

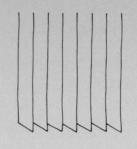

Narrow pleats all pressed in the same direction.

Tips for Perfect Pleats

■ Mark pleat lines carefully to assure they are straight and evenly spaced. Use thread, disappearing ink markers, pins, scissor clips, or other preferred method.

■ Manipulate, stitch, and press pleats as early as possible in the construction process, so you can work flat. As garment pieces are sewn together and the garment takes shape, it's more difficult to control the pleats.

■ Sew pleats from bottom to top, or wider to narrower, areas of the garment, to keep the pleated edge from stretching or rippling.

■ Stitch close to pleat edges on the inside of the garment, after the hem is finished, to hold pleats in place. You can also edgestitch pleat edges on the right side if you don't mind being able to see the stitching lines.

■ Stitch pleats far enough so they don't release at a wide point on your figure. Skirt pleats that release below a wide hipline are slimming because the fullness and swing of the skirt make the hips look small by comparison.

How to Press a Perfect Pleat

■ Insert strips of paper between the pleats when pressing, to prevent an imprint of the folded edge on the skirt fabric.

■ If you prefer basting pleats before pressing them, use silk thread, which doesn't leave an imprint.

■ Always use a pressing cloth to protect the fabric. The extra steam, time, and pressure required to set pleats can flatten the fabric's nap and leave an unwanted shine.

■ Steam well, and then use a tailor's clapper or other heavy weight to set pleats.

■ Always let pressed pleats dry and cool completely before removing from ironing surface or moving on to another section of pleating.

■ Don't do a final pressing of pleats at the lower edge until the hem is finished; then, you can set the pleats permanently.

■ To set pleats or trouser creases if steam isn't enough, spray or sponge the pressing cloth with a diluted solution of white vinegar and water. You can use a vinegar/water solution to remove creases, too; just spray or sponge, and press flat.

A Stitch in Time

To store fabric, roll around tubes or bolts to prevent hard-to-remove creases and fade lines. Or simply unfold the fabric and crinkle it up into a ball; you'd have to press it anyway before cutting.

before, and even fine materials such as silk and imported rayon can be delicately hand or machine washed in cold water. If you limit the fabrics that must be dry-cleaned, and favor those that you can launder at home, you won't begrudge their time away from your closet. When fabric-shopping, always check out the care instructions as you browse, so you don't miss a luscious material that can also be easily cared for. Always ask the sales staff how to care for a selected fabric before you leave the store, and jot down some reminder notes on the receipt. When you get home, attach a tag to the yardage and transfer these important care notes, so you will remember how to treat it when you finally get around to sewing it.

If, however, you always gravitate toward the fine wools, specialty silks, and other dry cleanables, plan a core wardrobe of key garments made out of them and then sew a good selection of companion garments out of easier-care cloth. Remember to mark these fabrics with care notes too, so you don't have to deal with a disaster later on, such as accidentally machine washing a dry-clean-only gabardine skirt. With a little planning, you can build a wardrobe of all your favorite styles and fabrics, yet without breaking your budget or creating garments that demand too much attention.

There are also many new high-tech fabrics coming out all the time, from microfiber to fleece, and each one has a different feel and look. Think about using some of these new miracle materials to update and refresh your wardrobe, and for the pure pleasure of trying something new. If you're unsure about how to sew with or care for some of these revolutionary new fibers, ask for guidance and ideas at your favorite fabric shop. Some stores even offer short courses or half-day workshops on special techniques for new products, such as fleece, slinky knits, Tencel, and hemp. If you are a lover of fabric, as most sewers are, your fingers will tingle with joy at the prospect of creating something beautiful with new materials.

COORDINATE THE NEW WITH THE OLD

While every fabric-buying jaunt is filled with promise and adventure, you'll get more mileage out of your sewing if you limit your search to fabrics that will coordinate with your already-made fashions back home. This is one of the

most difficult challenges all sewers face—to resist those
luscious, gorgeous lengths of fabric that, unfortunately,
don't go with anything else you have and would require
the manufacture of an entire companion wardrobe. Self-
discipline and the ability to lovingly fondle and then walk
away from those tempting fabrics will pay off, however, in
a versatile wardrobe that is well-balanced and complete. If
you purchase materials that harmonize with other items
hanging in your closet, then you won't waste time making
items that can be worn only by themselves. Of course, the
love of fabric and sewing is a passion, and every sewer
should occasionally surrender to that irresistible combination of fabric and pattern, to create an unparalleled one-of-
a-kind garment that glows all by itself in the closet.

If you are a fabric-aholic, also like most sewers, and just
keep bringing home more yardage, don't feel bad. Luckily,
cloth doesn't go sour or rot for a very long time, and it's
almost always a very good investment. The only risk is that
your changing tastes and preferences will turn your past
fabric purchases into current undesirables. If this happens
to some of your stash, you can wait until your tastes come
around again and add on another room to your home for
your growing inventory, or go ahead and open up some
storage space by using out-of-date cloth for pattern-testing,
quilting, samplers, home decorating items, or stuffing for
pillows. You can also organize a fabric swap with friends
or unload extra fabric at a flea market or yard sale.
Getting rid of unwanted fabric is not a usual occurrence,
but building up large inventories of fabric you don't use is
pretty common. And while fabric on shelves or in drawers
provides a warm and fuzzy sense of security, fabric made
up into clothing is far more gratifying. Therefore, put all
your fabric purchases to efficient work by choosing the
ones that dovetail with your past creations before you run
out of room to store any more.

ORGANIZE YOUR SPACE FOR EFFICIENT SEWING

Just as you put all available time slots to work making
progress on your sewing, you can learn to make efficient
use of all available nooks and crannies of space in your
home. Even if you live in cramped quarters or don't have
a dedicated sewing room, lack of space should not be a
reason to stop or cut back on your favorite activity. You
probably would love to have a larger kitchen, more closet
space, or a roomier office, but know it's just a dream.
Instead, you have probably learned how to organize the
space you do have and make the most of every little cub-
byhole and surface. You can do the same thing for all of
the various space needs common to sewing, and even
make some areas serve multiple purposes.

If you have a studio or sewing room, count your blessings
and enjoy the luxury of being able to cut, stitch, and press
in the same place. Then, organize your equipment and
supplies to match your preferred stitching habits. Arrange
cutting and marking supplies so they are right where you
need them; you won't waste time hunting for your shears
or rotary cutter. Keep handy notions within reach and the
ironing board just a step or swivel away. Hang up a bulletin board so you can see your latest collection of inspiration clippings, sketches, or photos; your creative mind can
be working up new ideas while you complete tedious tasks
at the machine. Display your inventory of fabric or swatches nearby, so you can be thinking about future garments or
unusual combinations of color and texture.

If you don't have the luxury of a dedicated sewing space,
evaluate your entire home for alcoves, corners, counter-
tops, and sub-spaces you can adapt to your particular
needs. Use the upper shelf of a closet to store bolts of fabric or an unused closet (is there such a thing?) for a sewing
or pressing alcove. Sections of the laundry area, basement, and even the bathroom can be reserved to store supplies and equipment or provide space for certain sewing-
related activities. Set aside a shelf in the pantry for cutting
tools or a desktop in the family room for your serger. Even
a corner of your bedroom can stow a basket or chest of
fabric, and a small section of wall can display some of
your personal inspiration materials or decorative embroidery samples.

On-Demand Space

You don't necessarily need everything to be in the same place to get your sewing done, as long as you organize what you need for any specific project or procedure. Different zones of your house can be designated for different sewing functions—cutting and marking, stitching, fitting, storage, etc. To bring it all together when you need it, put together a mobile sewing kit on wheels that can carry everything you need for a current project, and wheel it wherever you will complete the next step.

This simple, humble approach to gathering supplies can save significant amounts of time; you will avoid running back to the closet for a measuring tape or down to the basement for a spool of basting thread. Even a suitcase on casters or a child's wagon will do the trick, so you can consolidate what you need where and when you need it. A fishing tackle box, carpenter's toolbox and apron, computer case, child's toy box with handles, picnic basket, milk crate, laundry basket, or stacking baskets set on a wood base with casters all are ingenious, low-cost, double-duty solutions to the problem of limited sewing space. You might even think about making up a custom checklist that you can fill out for each sewing project, listing the various notions and accessories you will need; then simply gather the items in one trip around the house and put them in your mobile kit.

Organizing your supplies also ensures that you will be well stocked with what you need for your sewing projects, because an organized system makes it easier to see what you have and identify what you need. As you gather the equipment for a specific project, you can easily note items that are running low and then be sure to get more before you run out at an inconvenient time. Turn your custom checklist into a personalized inventory tracking system by also using it as a custom shopping list. Use that new computer program you are learning to design a practice document that lists all the essential equipment you must have on hand to be an efficient sewer. The list might include preferred interfacing, standard colors of thread, pattern tracing paper, marking pens, and more. Then, as you gather supplies for a particular project, check off items you will need to replace. Whatever inventory-tracking method you devise, the goal is to keep your sewing area well stocked so that your stitching progress is never hampered by lack of supplies.

Make Room for the Necessary Accessories

When you're not using notions and accessories, it's helpful to have efficient and handy storage spaces for them. After you roll them back to their permanent hiding places, ingenious storage solutions will keep them organized and ready for their next call to duty. Sewing stores and mail order catalogs offer good selections of nifty storage solutions, from pegboards to stacking trays. But if you don't have such sewing-specific storage gadgets, you can improvise and be ingenious with all kinds of bins, boxes, and baskets. Browse the hardware or discount stores when you're shopping for other needs and look for space-saving devices when scanning the latest interior design or kitchen supply catalogs. Stores that specialize in closet organization will yield compartmentalized bins that might be perfect for bobbins, threads, and other notions. Just as you studied the environment and passersby when collecting ideas for your inspiration library, you should keep your eyes open for simple containers and gadgets that can be put to multiple uses for your sewing convenience.

Don't Forget the Special Touches

Be sure to stake out a special corner, wall space, or portion of your mobile sewing kit for a special, inspirational touch that reminds you about why you love sewing. A changing selection from your idea resource library on a small bulletin board or several fabric swatches on the

Designer M. Luanne Carson turned a pair of plain black jeans into something special with these easy suede belt carriers. She simply clipped off the standard jean belt loops and used suede scraps to make interesting alternatives. Simple touches like this add a bit of pizzazz to plain garments, in a minimum of time.

refrigerator door can stimulate new ideas and keep you feeling fresh. Putting something that will inspire ideas, such as a sketch or swatch, right out in the open where you can see it whenever you pass by is especially helpful if your fabrics and supplies are stored away out of sight or distributed all over the house.

For comfort, invest in a small heater that fits under the sewing table or an ergonomically correct pillow to support you during long hours of dedicated stitching. Bright lights keep you alert and guard against stitching mistakes. A clock to keep you on schedule and a radio to keep you entertained will protect you from distractions that take you away from the garment you're trying so hard to finish up. A good mirror helps you evaluate fit accurately and shows off your beautiful creations. Find room for the small touches that warm your heart and provide a lift for tired eyes, from family photos to a mind-calming photo of a serene landscape. Such small but special touches increase your comfort, keep you on the stitching track, and remind you that sewing deserves a special place in your life.

LET NEW TECHNOLOGY IMPROVE YOUR SEWING

Just as new fabrics are being developed all the time, innovative notions and supplies are being invented to help you improve stitching skills or save time on particular steps. Many of these items are designed by busy sewers, who, like you, are always looking for ways to shave precious minutes off a time-consuming process or ease a complex operation. To continue to fit as much sewing as possible into your ever-busier schedule, review what's available and take advantage of every opportunity to increase efficiency or streamline the sewing process.

Sergers for home use were considered to be "extra" equipment not too long ago; now they are nearly standard in every sewing home because they so quickly perform various functions and therefore speed garment assembly. Rotary cutters were "revolutionary" just a few years ago and now they are the quick cutting method of choice for quilters and other sewers. Marking and basting aids, adhesives and fusibles, and other time- and labor-saving devices are continually designed and improved to help you get more sewing done. Computerized sewing machines and specialty machine attachments have trans-

formed sewing, making so much more possible than ever before. Keep up with what's available in the latest sewing magazines and mail order catalogs, at local and regional sewing exhibitions, and in the equipment and accessory departments of your favorite sewing shop. You will probably come across notions and aids that are perfect for the type of sewing you do and will help you improve quality or increase productivity.

IMPROVISE YOUR OWN HIGH TECH

Let the inventor in you flourish and look for ways to improvise your own time- and labor-saving technology, using what's already available for other purposes. For example, jewelry and dental tools make great aids for picking and manipulating short threads; surgical tools offer alternatives for precise cutting; kitchen accessories can do double duty for handy storage; and graphic arts supplies will work for marking and tracing. Fishing weights will add heft when and where you need it, and fly-tying supplies can be used for beautiful and unusual embellishment. Fashion your own pressing aids out of scraps from the wood workshop, and take advantage of computer and camera accessories for delicate machine-cleaning supplies.

NEVER STOP LEARNING

A natural companion to keeping up with new technology is identifying what can help you and learning how to properly and profitably use it. Experiment with new attachments or notions to get the most time- and labor-saving advantages out of their ingenious design. Review your sewing machine's capabilities every so often, to remind yourself of all it can do. As you test new sewing techniques, you may find a use for one of your machine's functions that you have previously ignored. Get out the owner's manual and selection of attachments that came with the machine, and review their performance. It's easy to get in a sewing rut, using the same machine functions to do the same old thing; an occasional self-education session will re-introduce you to the multi-faceted potential of your equipment. If your local fabric store offers a variety of classes or workshops, you might even suggest that they offer an occasional "New Product Showcase" or "Machine Review" that would help keep participants current with technological developments.

When rereading the owner's manual, review the accessories that your machine prefers and purchase only those types. Avoid substituting needles, sewing machine feet, or other attachments in a pinch or in an effort to save money. Today's highly sophisticated equipment is precisely designed to work well under the optimum conditions. Substituting other brands of accessories or trying to make a machine do something it wasn't designed to do may result in a breakdown that costs dearly to have repaired. Even more devastating is the possibility that you will be unable to sew for days, weeks, or months. Don't forget to review the basic maintenance steps your equipment requires to assure top-notch performance. Maintaining your supplies in tip-top shape guarantees that your sewing schedule will hum right along, undisturbed.

SEWING PREP STEPS

Getting ready to sew can often be a glitch in smooth, streamlined sewing production. Pretreating fabric, laying and cutting it out, and getting the pieces properly marked are often activities that get delayed over and over, because they are just not as much fun as dreaming about new creations or the actual construction of a new garment. Additionally, cutting out new patterns often requires rearranging the dining room or sewing area; on some evenings, that just seems like too big a job to get done before bedtime.

However, you can complete these necessary prep steps by using the same orderly, task-oriented techniques you apply to other activities. Schedule them with the same seriousness you use to reserve time for fabric-shopping or actual sewing, and fit these prep steps into your everyday routine. By working these activities into your daily schedule, you'll be assured of getting them done efficiently and having them completed when you're finally ready to sit and sew. For example, preshrink fabric, interfacing, and notions right along with or in between loads of family laundry, or while dinner is cooking. Don't pass on this important step, because sooner or later you will suffer the pain of sewing a wonderful fashion out of fresh, untreated fabric, only to see it come out of the wash several sizes smaller than intended.

Before you start cutting, review the pattern one more time and remind yourself about the changes you might be mak-

ing. For example, you might have decided to omit pockets or move the zipper placement; if so, it will be helpful to remember this right at the beginning, in case the variation will require a change in cutting or marking strategy. Or you may have rearranged the order of construction to accommodate your schedule for the week, or to create a stopping point so you can incorporate a creative technique; reminding yourself about this before you get started will keep you on track and moving smoothly toward completion. If you have made fitting alterations to the pattern, be sure to accurately mark adjustments before cutting it out, to be sure you end up with a perfectly fitting result. It's helpful to notate such changes right on the pattern instruction sheets, so you will remember the various adjustments or variations as you proceed from cutting area to sewing machine, and to guarantee that you won't have to backtrack during the construction process because you forgot to incorporate a change.

If the cutting out stage means a disruption of your living space, consider cutting several patterns out at once in assembly-line fashion, even if you don't plan to start sewing them right away. This saves time because you won't be rearranging furniture as often; it also creates a backlog of ready-to-go projects that will patiently wait for you to begin stitching them. You might want to choose two or three similar garments that can benefit from the same interfacing, lining, and thread. When cutting the interfacing for a pair of summer pants, maximize your efficiency by cutting out a similar pair for winter and cut the interfacing twice. Then, store the winter pair until you're ready to begin sewing for that season; the prep steps will already be completed, and you can jump right in on the stitching.

You can also use the cutting session for one garment as a testing session for new tools, techniques, or future gar-

---

A Stitch in Time

If you can't distinguish the right side from the wrong side of fabric, choose one or the other and mark it some way, to keep it consistent throughout garment construction.

ments. For example, practice using a new rotary cutter, try using weights to hold the pattern pieces down instead of pinning them to the fabric, or experiment with different marking tools. While the cutting board and tools are out, go ahead and cut the muslin pieces for making fitting samples of several new patterns; then, put them aside until you're ready to pretest the patterns. Cut and test several samplers of fusible interfacing and fashion fabric combinations that you can use as reference for future projects. Or cut the bias strips of various different fabrics for interesting bias edgings that might eventually get paired up with a future garment.

Before dismantling the cutting area, be sure all pattern pieces are correctly and accurately marked. Notches, dots, and other identifying marks are critical to successful garment construction, so don't neglect this important step. Components that are completely marked will be easily aligned and the assembly process will be smooth and untroubled. Experiment with the many marking techniques until you find the one that matches your style and is the most speedy. Try out the various chalks and pens for marking, or use pins, scissor clips, or thread to indicate notches, darts, and other important points.

TIPS FOR SPEED SEWING

Once all prep steps have been completed, you will be ready to fly when you finally get to the sewing machine. If you have prepared a "Plan for the Week," like those in this book, you can tell at a glance what your goals are for each session. If you know ahead of time what you want to get done, it will be easier to find the time to complete the designated tasks. For example, if you want to be sure that a beautifully embroidered garment is ready to wear by Monday morning, organize the preparation and construction tasks for the prior week; you will be more likely to set aside enough time to complete the embroidery far enough in advance that finishing up will be no problem. If you have extra time after any one sewing session, you're free to move to the next step, get ready for the next project, or take time away from the machine and inspire yourself by changing the selection of images on your inspiration bulletin board.

The "Plan for the Week" also helps you organize every sewing project into smaller, manageable tasks that can be easily completed according to the amount of time or energy you have available. Review the pattern and reorganize the construction steps to match your schedule. You don't have to follow the order written out by the manufacturer, especially if you're already familiar with the pattern and how it goes together. Instead, group similar steps together regardless of their sequence in the pattern instructions, or segment other more complicated steps and spread them out over two evenings if you know you will be short on time. You can also reorganize construction according to the type of procedure you will be doing. For example, group tedious steps so you can get them over with in the same evening or else combine them with other, more fun tasks and spread out over several evenings. If you're particularly tired on one evening, skip the preplanned step and, instead, do something that will perk you up, such as making a sampler of decorative stitching, experimenting with fabric piecing, rearranging fabric swatches, or simply taking the night off. When you schedule the construction process ahead of time, you'll feel more comfortable taking a night off if you feel confident that you'll still be able to complete the project by the desired date.

Your own sewing experience has probably exposed you to many shortcuts and tips; many others can be found in the pages of this and other books, from sewing friends, and in classes. While it's difficult to break personal sewing habits, it's worth trying out some shortcuts and new ways of doing things, to see if they will improve the quality of your stitching or speed up garment construction. When you're getting ready to move on to a particular procedure, such as a fly-front pants opening, take a break and look it up in the various books or magazines in your personal library. Review the various recommendations for quick and easy fly fronts, and then proceed with the one that makes the most sense for your sewing style. This is the perfect time to try out an alternative method, when you can practice on a real garment, because it is unlikely that you will devote precious sewing time to experimentation for its own sake.

Do not, however, take any shortcuts on the pressing part of sewing. Pressing is extremely important to garment assembly and its final appearance. Arrange your sewing area so that the ironing board is close by and the iron is ready to go at a moment's notice, and press step by step as you go. To optimize efficiency, some sewers keep the iron turned on all the time during every sewing session, so they

The Zipper:
Essential Accessory

If someone asked you to endure an entire day without using that neat little contraption called the zipper, could you do it? Open a dresser drawer and you'd probably have trouble finding a pair of pants without it. Reach into the coat closet on a blustery morning and chances are you'd end up empty-handed. Even grabbing a purse or money belt to pay for gas would most likely mean pulling the tab of this universal slide-fastening device.

Despite its prevalence in the late 20th century, the earliest version of the modern-day zipper did not enjoy such immense popularity. In fact, proponents of the first marketed "hookless fastener" battled skeptical fashion designers, reluctant clothing manufacturers, and dissatisfied consumers for nearly 40 years before becoming an accepted part of everyday life.

The first recorded invention similar to the modern zipper hailed from Elias Howe, father of the sewing machine. He patented his "automatic continuous clothing closure" in 1851. However, the concept of a "series of clasps united by a connecting cord running or sliding upon ribs" was not actually marketed until the end of the 19th century. In 1893, the innovative mechanical engineer Whitcomb Judson patented two versions of "certain new and useful Improvements in Clasp Lockers and Unlockers for Shoes, &c." His designs would later become the zipper as we know it today.

As Judson's original name reveals, the first metal slide closures were intended to simplify the arduous task of fastening dozens of buttons on high-buttoned shoes, the most fashionable and practical style of footwear found in the unpaved streets of the late 19th century. Even though the buttoned shoe slide fastener never quite caught on in a big way, a later footwear style eventually propelled the invention to a high degree of popularity and gave it its modern name as well.

The B.F. Goodrich Company ordered an overwhelming 170,000 slide fasteners in 1923 and began to market the Mystik Boot, a style of rubber galoshes that opened and closed with the patented Hookless Fastener. Dissatisfied with the name, which he considered impractical, Goodrich President Bertram G. Work suggested a more active label, such as "zip," after the sound the slide fastener made when putting on the boots. "Why not call it the zipper?" he

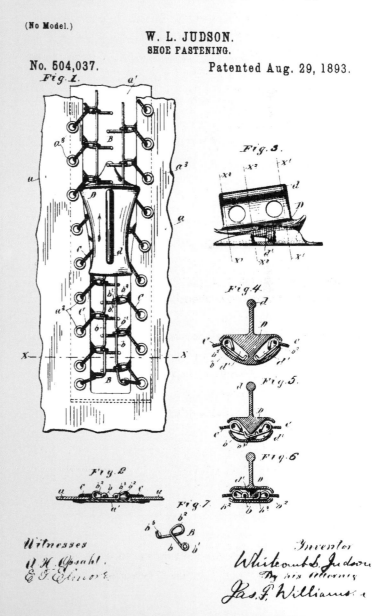

(No Model.)

W. L. JUDSON.
SHOE FASTENING.

No. 504,037.

Patented Aug. 29, 1893.

wondered, having no idea of the widespread generic use the result of his sudden brainstorm would have in future decades.

Despite the success of the Zipper Boot, manufacturers of the Hookless Fastener endured another decade of hopeful advertising schemes and product improvements before the newfangled device would shake off its status as a novelty item and join the ranks of everyday conveniences. Zipper makers bombarded the clothing industry with advertisements in the late 1920s, even promoting the zipper as a tool for child psychology. Ads in parenting magazines proposed that if children wore Self-Dress clothing, they would learn independence and self-reliance as they zipped up.

By the mid-1930s, the zipper had become a common household sight in overalls, playsuits, hunting jackets, galoshes, and handbags. However, it did not make significant inroads into high fashion until 1937, when an unexpected demand for men's summer suits surprised zipper makers and confirmed the success of their persistent advertising campaigns. Some believe that trendsetter Edward, the Duke of Windsor, contributed to the new rage, when he began wearing zippered fashions.

On the women's clothing front, zippers made even bigger news when the flashy Parisian designer Elsa Schiaparelli caught reporters and buyers off guard with her 1935 spring collection. The models wore gowns and dresses splashed with colorful zippers made of plastic, the newest innovation in fasteners.

In an age hooked on slim lines, American zipper makers aimed to convince women that the device was an instant path to a thin figure. Zippered girdles and corsets were touted as necessary complements to the sleek, full-length coats and streamlined, clingy dresses on the fashion runways. Advertisers of Talon fasteners (the original Hookless Fastener manufacturer) made a lasting impression with their famous "Gap-osis" campaign, which pictured women with pronounced gaps between the bulging buttons in the plackets of their garments, and warned them of the impropriety and unfashionable taste of fashions made without Talon fasteners. "It's no laughing matter to have 'gap-osis,' a show-off placket," one persuasive advertisement read.

"Especially nowadays, when everybody's attention is on neat little waistlines."

The zipper craze of the late 1930s established the zipper as the norm rather than the exception in clothing styles and other items. Manufacturers of the hookless fastener had finally succeeded in convincing private industry and the public that their product was more than just a passing fad.

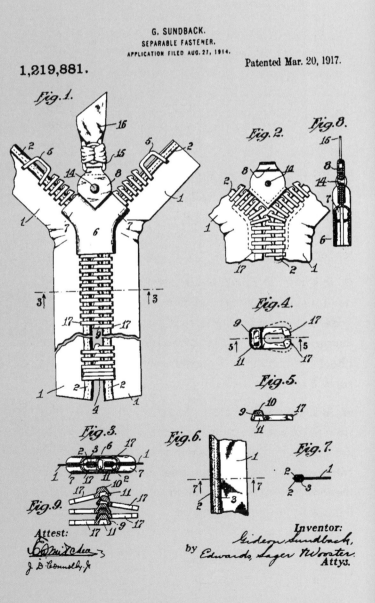

G. SUNDBACK.
SEPARABLE FASTENER.
APPLICATION FILED AUG. 27, 1914.

1,219,881.

Patented Mar. 20, 1917.

Putting in zippers can be a little tricky. In fact, every sewer has had her own experience with various glitches, from putting a zipper in upside down or inside out to accidentally cutting off the pull tab. Before stitching a zipper into a garment, it is always helpful to take a deep breath, focus your attention, and remember these helpful hints.

■ Serge or finish the raw edges of the seam allowances before inserting the zipper, for a clean finish and neat effect. It's much easier to do this before the zipper is stitched in place.

■ Use narrow strips of interfacing to stabilize zipper seam allowances, to prevent rippling or uneven seams. This is particularly helpful for bias fabrics that can easily stretch out of shape.

■ Carefully position the zipper so the teeth will align exactly with the seam opening. Baste or temporarily hold in place with tape, glue, or fusible web before you stitch.

■ Just because the pattern calls for a particular zipper length doesn't mean you can't use a different one, especially if it eases getting into and out of a skirt or pair of slacks. Just be sure to leave enough seam open for a longer zipper or stitch it up for a shorter one.

■ To shorten a zipper, make a new zipper stop by hand sewing or machine stitching a bar tack (a wide, short zigzag) across the teeth just below the desired length. Cut off the extra length about ½" (1.25 cm) below the bar tack, carefully clipping between the teeth.

■ To shorten a fly front zipper, cut off from the top, leaving the original zipper bottom at the notch or dot and stitching a bar tack on each side at the top. Be careful not to cut off the pull tab when trimming off the extra length.

■ To make sure the stitching is even and equally spaced on each side of the zipper, baste the zipper in place and then stitch it from the right side of the garment. It will be easier to see exactly where the zipper opening is and where your stitching lines must go.

■ To avoid crooked stitching lines as you sew around the pull tab, lower the needle into the fabric, lift the presser foot, and carefully push or pull the tab out of the way. Lower the presser foot and continue stitching a straight and even line. An alternative is to use a longer zipper; push the tab all the way off the edge of the fabric, stitch zipper in place, lower tab back onto garment, sew a bar tack on each side, and cut off excess zipper tape.

■ For a smooth and flat seam, stitch both sides of the zipper from bottom to top, in two steps.

■ For the most invisible stitching, hand stitch the zipper in place, using small back stitches, and don't pull the stitches too tight. Machine stitching is quicker, but it's also visible and leaves impressions in the fabric. Looser hand stitches will barely make an impression and will hardly show, which may be worth the few extra minutes required.

■ Try not to press the zipper teeth, especially with a hot iron. Instead, lightly press the seam on either side, just up to the teeth.

CREATIVE COVER-UPS

SEWING DISASTERS CAN BE OPPORTUNITIES FOR A CREATIVE FIX. IN THIS SKIRT, DESIGNER MARY PARKER ACCIDENTALLY USED THE POCKET LINING PATTERN PIECE TO CUT THE SIDE FRONT, RESULTING IN A TOO-SMALL SECTION. SHE WONDERS WHETHER, AFTER A LIFETIME OF WORKING WITH FABRIC, OTHER SEWERS STILL MAKE MISTAKES LIKE THIS ONE. MARY DIDN'T HAVE ENOUGH FABRIC TO RECUT THE SIDE FRONT PIECES, SO SHE HAD TO RESORT TO CREATIVE INGENUITY TO FINISH THE SKIRT. SHE USED LEFTOVER SCRAPS OF FABRIC TO CUT SMALL WEDGES, BUTTED THEM NEXT TO THE WRONGLY-CUT SIDE FRONTS, AND SECURED THEM ON THE BACK SIDE WITH FUSIBLE INTERFACING. THEN, SHE TOPPED OFF THE JOIN WITH A BIAS STRIP OF SELF-FABRIC. THE RESULT IS A CONTRASTING STRIP THAT ECHOES THE ANGLE OF THE POCKET. NO ONE WOULD EVER KNOW THERE WAS A MISTAKE UNDERNEATH, BECAUSE IT LOOKS AS IF MARY PLANNED IT JUST THAT WAY.

don't have to wait for it to warm up (be sure to keep an eye on the water reservoir if you do this), and others lower the board to sitting height and position it adjacent to the machine so they don't have to get up to press a seam. When shopping for fabric, take a few moments to browse the notions department for handy pressing aids or efficient new irons; some new products may enhance your sewing productivity.

FINISHING TOUCHES MAKE THE DIFFERENCE

Adding a special finishing touch to a basic, simple pattern is one of the easiest ways to quickly create a unique fashion. Such special effects can be achieved in many different ways and at different stages of garment assembly. For example, different fabric manipulation techniques can be implemented before construction even begins, such as piecing or pleating custom yardage. Garment components can be redesigned for interest, such as contouring a hemline or adding shaped insertions to seams. During assembly, style lines can be enhanced with edgings and piping, draped overlays or appliqués can be added, or facings can be reversed and shaped for interest. Once the garment is completed, you can treat the finished product as a starting point for all manner of embellishments, from decorative buttons or beadwork to applied trims or inventive accessories.

Finishing touches can be planned in advance or thought up after the garment is fully made up, in response to the observation, "This piece needs something else." If you know what the special effect will be right at the outset, be sure to add reminder notes to the pattern instructions so you won't forget to stop where appropriate in order to incorporate the effect. For example, if you know you will be adding decorative braid along the outseams of a pair of slacks, you can plan ahead to hide the raw ends within seam allowances before stitching the seams or attaching the waistband.

If you wait to be inspired until after the garment is sewn, hang it up where you can see it and wait for the perfect idea to suggest itself. The crowning touch might be as simple as some artful buttons, a sequined accent, or carefully placed embroidery motif. Don't forget to include scarves, jewelry, other accessories, and various companion garments as possible partners for a fabulous finished look.

A Stitch in Time

Don't panic when something goes wrong. Take a breather, and then solve the problem creatively. It's likely that no one but you will ever know you had to devise a quick fix.

SEWING REPAIR SHOP

Despite your most thorough planning and careful attention, accidents occasionally do happen in the sewing room, and you probably have had your own share of disastrous mishaps. Misfortunes can include miscalculating the amount of needed yardage, an accidental slip of the shears, stitching wrong parts together, or slicing through a buttonhole bar tack. Whether these stitching casualties are minor or severe, they all cause an immediate sinking feeling in the stomach and the occasional question, "Why do I bother to sew at all?" However, with a little creative ingenuity, almost all accidents can be repaired so that most observers would never know that something went wrong.

The first stage in your repair strategy is simple grieving. Take a deep breath, turn off the machine, put the scissors away, and leave the room. Leave the wounded project alone for a while, or overnight, and let your anger and frustration subside. When you come back to it, you'll be able to assess the damage and devise a solution with a clear head. You might be able to buy a little more of the same yardage, recut the piece, and proceed as usual. You may have to redesign the garment, omitting patch pockets or substituting different fabric for the facings. An extreme solution may be to cut the injured garment apart and recycle the fabric in another piece or a quilt. If the accident was cataclysmic, you may find it comforting to shred the garment and throw it away; at least, you'll be freed of the evidence and can move on to something else.

But before you give up on the possibility of rehabilitation, exercise your creative faculties in an attempt to camouflage the accident. Applied trims and appliqués will cover up a multitude of sins and, when strategically placed, will appear as if you designed the finished garment exactly that way. Beads, decorative buttons, embroidery motifs, decals, and other interesting graphics can also be effective disguises and look as if they have an intended purpose. Sashes, draped overlays, and other innovative overgarments can turn a near disaster into inspired art-to-wear. If you craft a clever cover-up, no one will ever know you had to resort to the repair toolbox. Observers will assume the garment turned out the way you planned it. So, take another deep breath, smile, and wear it with pride in your creative professionalism.

PICK A POCKET
for creative flair

If you're looking for a quick and easy way to add some novelty to a basic pattern, think about experimenting with pocket treatments. The pockets shown here demonstrate how designer M. Luanne Carson had a lot of fun playing around with fabric, notions, trim—and even hardware. Garments with unusual special effects like these really stand out from the crowd!

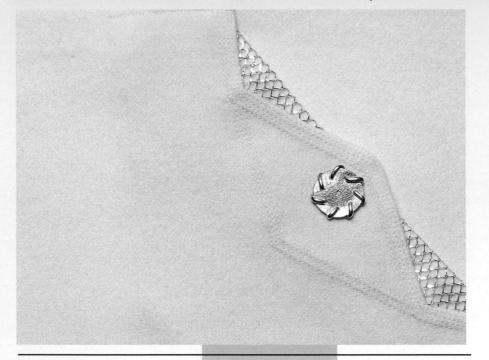

BELOW, TAKE ADVANTAGE OF THE SUBTLE DIFFERENCE BETWEEN THE TWO SIDES OF A FABRIC FOR DECORATIVE INTEREST. IN THIS VARIATION, THE DESIGNER OVERLAID THE SHAPED POCKET OPENING WITH A LAYER OF THE CREPE-BACK SATIN'S SHINY SIDE AND ACCENTED THE DIVIDING LINE WITH A ROW OF SHINY BEADS. THE BIAS EDGING AT THE OPENING PUFFED UP TO GIVE A TRAPUNTO RELIEF EFFECT.

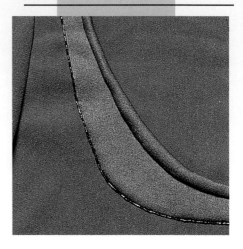

ABOVE, THE DESIGNER SHAPED THIS POCKET OPENING TO FORM A "W" AND THEN ADDED SEVERAL ROWS OF TOPSTITCHING FOR INTEREST. SHE COVERED A BAND OF SELF-FABRIC WITH A GLITTERING GOLD WEBBING AND LIGHTLY HAND-TACKED THE BAND BEHIND THE POCKET OPENING; THE BAND ENDS ARE SECURED IN THE SIDE AND WAIST SEAMS. TOPPED OFF WITH A DECORATIVE BUTTON, THIS POCKET IS TRULY ONE-OF-A-KIND.

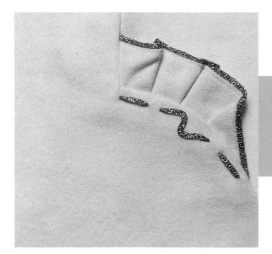

LEFT, THE DESIGNER TURNED A SIMPLE RECTANGLE OF FABRIC INTO THIS DRESSY DECORATION BY TRIMMING IT WITH GOLD BRAID AND FAN-PLEATING IT TO FIT THE POCKET OPENING. SHE REARRANGED THE FOLDS TO GET AN ATTRACTIVE EFFECT, STITCHED IT IN PLACE, AND THEN ADDED THE MEANDERING SIGNATURE OF GOLD BRAID AS AN ACCENT. A FLATTERING BONUS: THE UPWARD DIRECTION OF THE POCKET DECORATION LEADS THE OBSERVING EYE UP AND AWAY FROM THE HIPLINE.

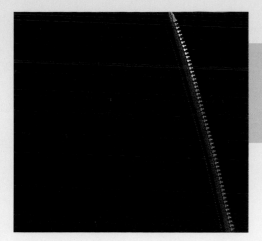

LEFT, PUT ZIPPERS TO INGENIOUS USE FOR THEIR DECORATIVE EFFECT, AS IN THIS VARIATION. THE DESIGNER TOPSTITCHED A SEPARATING ZIPPER ALONG THE OPENING OF A STANDARD SLANT POCKET AND LET THE BRIGHT RED ZIPPER TAPE SHOW, FOR A SPLASH OF COLOR. IF YOU USE ZIPPERS FOR CREATIVE INTEREST, CUT OFF BULKY HARDWARE AND CAREFULLY HAND-WALK THE SEWING MACHINE NEEDLE OVER ZIPPER TEETH WHEN STITCHING INTERSECTING SEAMS.

BELOW, FOR THIS FUN AND EASY POCKET VARIATION, THE DESIGNER CUT AN ELONGATED SELF-FABRIC SHAPE AND FINISHED THE RAW EDGES IN CONTRASTING THREAD. SHE THEN STITCHED ACROSS THE MIDDLE OF THE SHAPE INTO THE WELL OF THE WAISTLINE SEAM AND FLIPPED THE UPPER END DOWN. THIS SIMPLE DECORATION IS ALSO SLENDERIZING, BECAUSE OBSERVERS NOTICE THE INTERESTING SPECIAL EFFECT INSTEAD OF THE HIPLINE SILHOUETTE.

BELOW, HARDWARE IS AN UNCONVENTIONAL, BUT EXCITINGLY DIFFERENT, FINISHING TOUCH TO THIS SLANT POCKET. THE DESIGNER CONNECTED A D-RING AND TWO SWIVEL HOOKS TO FLUFFY CHENILLE YARN THAT IS STITCHED INTO THE SIDE AND WAIST SEAMS. THE POCKET OPENING IS FURTHER ACCENTED WITH A BLACK/WHITE RIBBON TRIM. INSPIRATION FOR DECORATIVE TREATMENTS CAN COME FROM ANYWHERE, EVEN THE HARDWARE STORE!

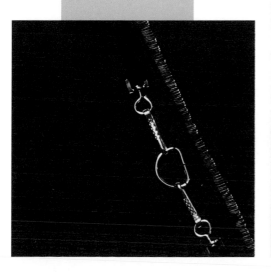

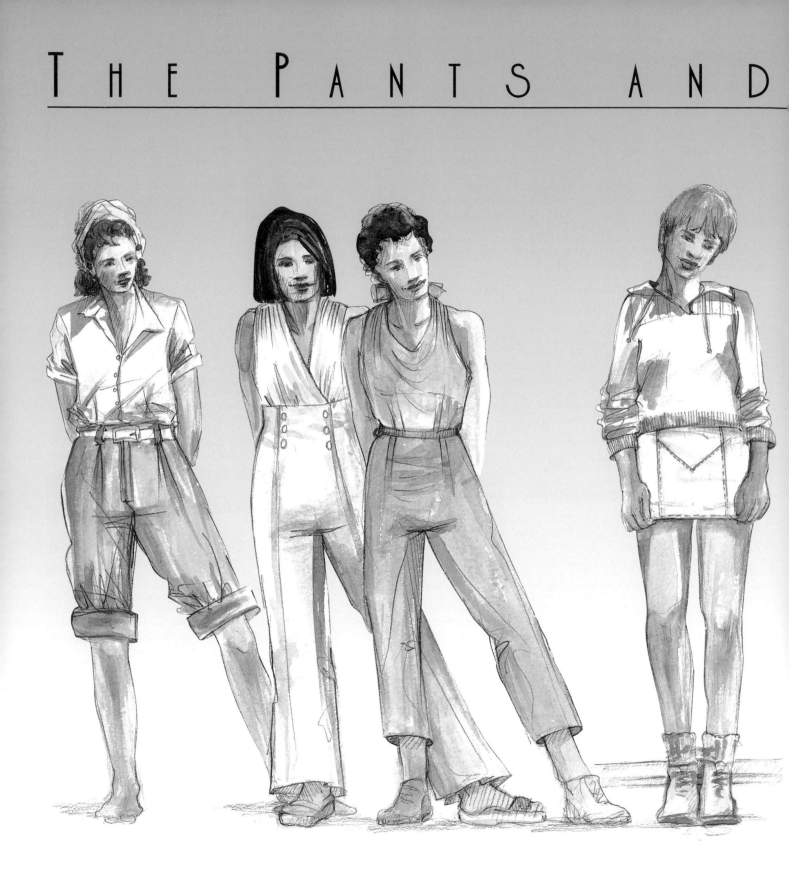

S KIRTS

Joined-at-the-Hip Pants
DESIGNER
Joyce Baldwin

Eliminate figure-widening bulk by transforming standard trousers into a sleek fashion without side seams.

DESIGN DETAILS

The designer started with a standard pleated pants pattern that featured slant pockets in the front. While she's a confirmed "pocket person," she doesn't like the bulk at the waist and hip that inseam pockets create. Therefore, she devised this way of reducing bulk at the side seam and repositioning different pocket designs to suit her. The result is a no-side-seam fashion that slims the figure without sacrificing the convenience of pockets.

CONSTRUCTION DETAILS

1. To join the pants at the hip, position the side front pattern piece under the front pattern piece, matching symbols. See Figure 1. Pin or tape temporarily.

2. Overlap the side seam stitching lines of the front and back pattern pieces at the widest part of the hip. See Figure 2. Pin or tape temporarily.

3. Measure the distance between the lengthwise grainlines on the front and back pattern pieces at this widest point. Continue to overlap the side seams all the way down to the lower edges of the pattern pieces, maintaining the measured distance between grainlines. Keeping the grainlines parallel to each other will eliminate any flair at the lower garment edge, in the hem area. Pin or tape pattern pieces together temporarily.

4. Cut out the joined front and back pattern pieces from wide fabric. NOTE: The fabric width must equal or exceed the widest point of the taped-together pattern, including seam allowances. The fabric width for these size 10 pants was 57" (145 cm). The original side seam area from the waist to hip will now be stitched as a curved dart, following the original stitching lines. See Figure 3. The dart will be very wide, so you may want to trim off some of the excess dart inside the garment and press it open to evenly distribute the fabric bulk.

5. Make double welt pockets in the front pieces before sewing the inseams. The pockets shown here are 6" (15 cm) long. They are positioned 2" (5 cm) below the waist seam stitching line; the top of the pocket is 1¼" (3 cm) in from the original side seam and the bottom is 2" (5 cm) in from the original side seam.

6. Complete pants according to pattern instructions.

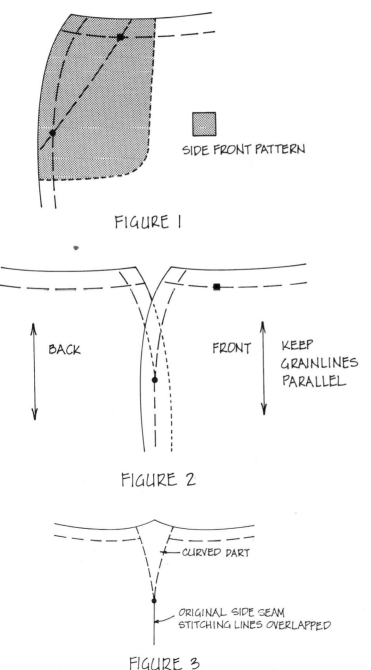

FIGURE 1

SIDE FRONT PATTERN

BACK   FRONT   KEEP GRAINLINES PARALLEL

FIGURE 2

CURVED DART

ORIGINAL SIDE SEAM STITCHING LINES OVERLAPPED

FIGURE 3

Tips from the designer

■ This design works particularly well for heavier fabrics, such as corduroy. Heavy fabrics can really bulk up in side seam allowances, especially where pocket seams intersect side seams. By eliminating the side seams and moving the pockets to the front, the bulk is removed and the hip area appears sleek and slim.

■ Pants alterations are often made at the side seams, but remember that the pattern modification shown here eliminates side seams except at the waist area. Therefore, make sure your original pattern fits you perfectly through the hip area before omitting side seams. You will still be able to alter the waist after modifying the pattern, however, by adjusting the size or curve of the dart.

■ No-side-seam fashions are a dream for plaids and other fabrics that require matching. The tedious and time-consuming task of lining up plaids or patterns at the side seam is totally eliminated!

■ This pattern modification works well for skirts, too, as long as you can find fabric wide enough.

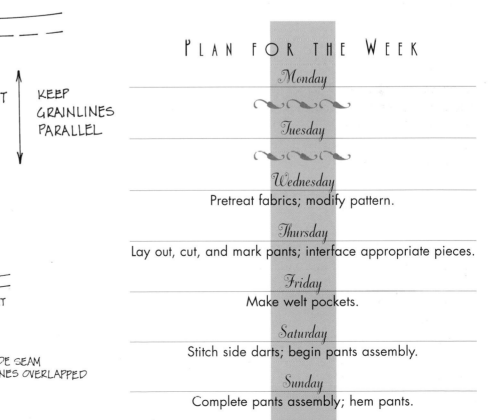

PLAN FOR THE WEEK

Monday

Tuesday

Wednesday
Pretreat fabrics; modify pattern.

Thursday
Lay out, cut, and mark pants; interface appropriate pieces.

Friday
Make welt pockets.

Saturday
Stitch side darts; begin pants assembly.

Sunday
Complete pants assembly; hem pants.

THIS BELLOWS POCKET EXPANDS TO ACCOMMODATE THE CONTENTS, AND LOOKS INTERESTING EVEN WHEN EMPTY AND FLAT AGAINST THE GARMENT. GUSSETS AROUND THREE SIDES ARE CREASED AND EDGESTITCHED TO FORM THE EXPANDABLE POCKET BAG. THEN, THE POCKET OPENING CAN BE VARIED WITH SNAPS, BUTTONHOLES AND BUTTONS, HOOK-AND-LOOP TAPE, FROGS OR OTHER DECORATIVE CLOSURES, OR A POCKET FLAP.

THE WAIST-TO-HIP DART REPLACES THE ORIGINAL SIDE SEAM OF A STANDARD PANTS PATTERN, AND CAN BE CURVED OR NARROWED TO ACCURATELY FIT THE WAIST. THE ORIGINAL SLANT POCKET IN THE SIDE SEAM WAS CHANGED TO A WELT POCKET IN THE FRONT, REMOVING UNWANTED BULK FROM THE HIP AREA.

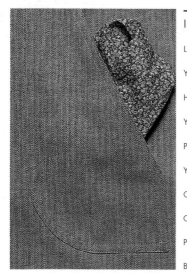

IF YOU'RE A POCKET PERSON, YOU LIKE THESE HANDY FEATURES ON ALL YOUR GARMENTS, WHETHER FOR HOLDING CAR KEYS OR PARKING YOUR HANDS. ONCE YOU TAKE POCKETS OUT OF THE SIDE SEAM, YOU ELIMINATE EXTRA BULK AND OPEN UP LOTS OF OPPORTUNITY FOR CREATIVE VARIATION. THIS SHAPED PATCH POCKET WAS SIMPLE TO MAKE, BY USING THE ORIGINAL PATTERN FOR THE POCKET LINING AS A CUTTING GUIDE. STITCH IT TO A LINING, TURN, PRESS, AND TOPSTITCH IN PLACE WHERE DESIRED.

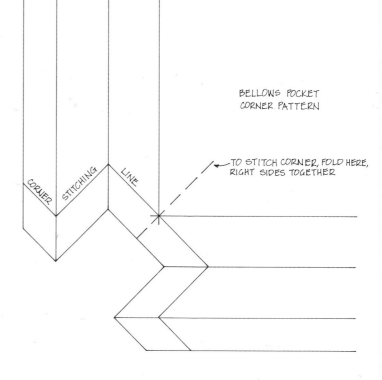

BELLOWS POCKET
CORNER PATTERN

CORNER STITCHING LINE

TO STITCH CORNER, FOLD HERE, RIGHT SIDES TOGETHER

Celestial Style
DESIGNER
M. Luanne Carson

The colors and sun motifs in this zodiac print inspired a gold grosgrain ribbon detail down the front that is also a vertical, figure-lengthening feature.

DESIGN DETAILS

The designer started with a simple pull-on pants pattern and added her own creative galaxy of special effects.

■ She first split the front leg from waist to hem, adding allowances for new vertical seams that break up the horizontal width of the figure and add visual length to the leg.

■ She then stitched grosgrain ribbon into the new seam for a nice graphic contrast with the print fabric, selected buttons that reflect the sun designs, and sewed them on in a decorative arrangement.

■ Since these pants are a pull-on style, the buttons are not functional. However, they certainly add pizzazz and glitter. Positioning the top buttons right on top of the waistband is good for a figure with a long waist, because they fill in a bit of the waist area, and visually reduce some of the distance between the upper and lower parts of the body.

One-Hour Skirt

DESIGNER
Marion E. Mathews

From fabric stash to finished wearable in a flash! No pattern needed—just cut two colorful skirt-length panels and elasticize a waistband for a fast and easy fit.

MATERIALS AND SUPPLIES

■ 1 yard (.95 m) fabric, 45" (1.1 m) wide

■ Waistband elastic, 1" (2.5 cm) wide

CONSTRUCTION DETAILS

1. Cut off the folded edge of the fabric, so you have two 1-yard (.95 m) pieces.

2. With right sides together, stitch long side edges of fabric to form a tube. Press seams open. Designate waist and hem edges.

3. Finish raw waist edge and turn under 1½" (4 cm). Stitch close to finished raw edge and ¼" (6 mm) from top folded edge, to form casing for elastic.

4. Cut elastic 3-4" (7.5-10 cm) smaller than your waistline measurement. Cut elastic piece in half.

5. Open up enough stitching at the side seams inside the waist to insert elastic pieces.

6. Thread one piece of elastic through the front casing and the other piece through the back, distributing gathers evenly. Butt ends of elastic and zigzag together, using a scrap of seam binding behind the join as a foundation. Slip stitch side seams closed.

7. Finish raw hem edge and turn up a 1" (2.5 cm) hem. Topstitch in place.

Tips from the designer

■ Be sure to choose a fluid, drapey fabric for this quick skirt, so it will gather nicely and not be too bulky around the waist.

■ With just a little extra time, you can add inseam pockets in the side seams (see page 89 for details). Cut the pockets out of coordinating lightweight fabric or lining so you don't have to purchase any more than 1 yard (.95 m) of the skirt fabric.

■ It's difficult to tell the front from the back on a skirt with an elasticized waist, so I always make a few hand stitches on the inside of the waistband at center back to make sure the skirt hangs well and side seam pockets are correctly positioned. This is especially important if you have to alter the backs or fronts of your skirts for an asymmetrical figure.

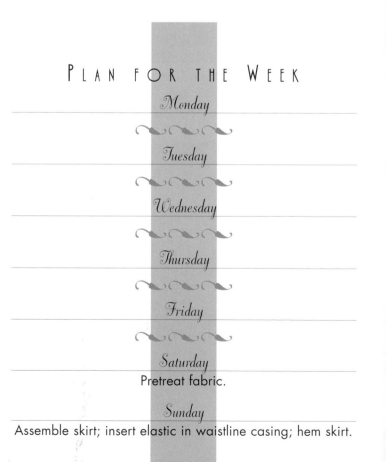

PLAN FOR THE WEEK

Monday

Tuesday

Wednesday

Thursday

Friday

Saturday
Pretreat fabric.

Sunday
Assemble skirt; insert elastic in waistline casing; hem skirt.

A FEW QUICK HAND STITCHES INSIDE
THE WAISTBAND MAKE IT A SNAP TO TELL
BACK FROM FRONT. THEN, YOU KNOW
THE SKIRT WILL HANG CORRECTLY WHEN
YOU WEAR IT.

Style Under Control

DESIGNER
Mary S. Parker

If your waistline measurements change during the day or month, a built-in tummy control panel will ensure that pleated pants look good anytime.

MATERIALS AND SUPPLIES

■ Pattern for pants, preferably one with a side front extension to the center front (see Figure 1 for modifying pattern without extension)

■ Tissue paper or pattern tracing paper

■ Fabric of choice

■ Approximately ½ yard (.5 m) Lycra, girdle, or other similar all-over stretch fabric

■ Notions required by pattern

CONSTRUCTION DETAILS

1. Trace a copy of the extended side front pattern piece onto extra paper.

2. Cut the copy along the line indicated in Figure 1 and add seam allowances to both cut edges.

3. Cut two curved pocket portions out of the selected fashion fabric; cut two extension portions from stretch girdle fabric.

4. Stitch fabric and stretch sections along cut line, with right sides together. Press seam to the fashion fabric side and topstitch in place.

5. Place original side front pattern piece on top of fabric/stretch piece and trim fabric to fit pattern piece exactly.

6. Repeat for other side.

7. Construct pants up to zipper insertion.

8. Baste front edge of stretch panel to pants front ¼" (6 mm) in from center front line, keeping edge of stretch panel parallel to center front.

9. Insert zipper and remove basting.

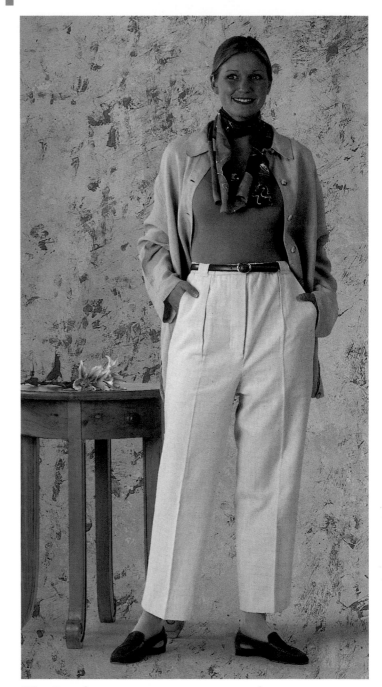

10. Complete pants construction, according to pattern guide sheet.

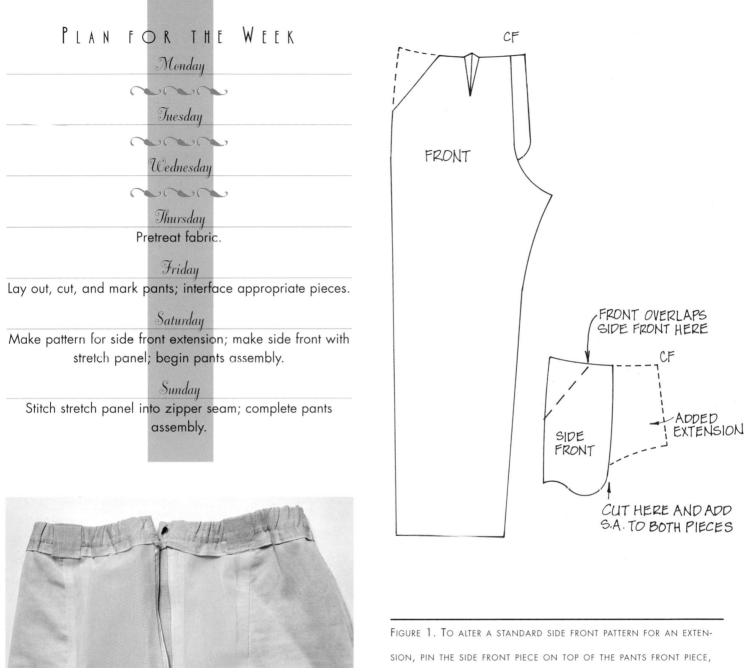

PLAN FOR THE WEEK

Monday

Tuesday

Wednesday

Thursday
Pretreat fabric.

Friday
Lay out, cut, and mark pants; interface appropriate pieces.

Saturday
Make pattern for side front extension; make side front with stretch panel; begin pants assembly.

Sunday
Stitch stretch panel into zipper seam; complete pants assembly.

A STRETCH FABRIC TUMMY-CONTROL PANEL HELPS KEEP PLEATED PANTS SMOOTH IN FRONT, DESPITE FLUCTUATIONS IN WAIST MEASUREMENT. THE STRETCH PANEL IS SIMPLY EXTENDED FROM THE SIDE FRONT POCKET PIECE TO CENTER FRONT.

FIGURE 1. TO ALTER A STANDARD SIDE FRONT PATTERN FOR AN EXTENSION, PIN THE SIDE FRONT PIECE ON TOP OF THE PANTS FRONT PIECE, MATCHING NOTCHES AND THE OVERLAP LINE. PIN PLEATS CLOSED ON FRONT PIECE AND FOLD UNDER THE FLY FRONT EXTENSION ALONG THE CENTER FRONT LINE. TAPE ADDITIONAL TISSUE OR PATTERN TRACING PAPER ON TOP OF THE SIDE FRONT PATTERN; TRACE THE OUTLINE OF THE TOP EDGE AND CENTER FRONT TO THE BOTTOM OF THE FLY. FROM THE BOTTOM OF THE FLY, DRAW A STRAIGHT OR SLIGHTLY CURVED LINE BACK TO THE ORIGINAL SIDE FRONT PATTERN.

Classic Skirt with a Twist
DESIGNER
Judith Robertson

No matter how basic your wardrobe, you can always come up with creative ideas for a different twist, like these knotted belt carriers.

DESIGN DETAILS

This designer works with a skeleton selection of basic pattern styles, so she can spend her hard-earned money on fabrics instead of more patterns. To satisfy her need for creative expression, she thinks up ingenious touches that make each garment in her wardrobe a unique version of a pattern she's made before. And to satisfy her requirement for practicality, she also makes adjustments to her patterns to ensure easy care and long wear.

■ These nifty belt carriers couldn't be easier. Just make a loose overhand knot in the carrier or belt loop before stitching it into the waistline seam. Don't forget to cut the carriers a little longer, because the knot can take up a surprising bit of length.

■ The designer loves special buttons and considers them important elements of a garment's overall look and quality. However, she dreads the idea of putting fine buttons through the wash or dry cleaning cycle. Therefore, she makes her own detachable buttons by sewing them to inexpensive, clear buttons with a long shank. Then, she makes a double set of buttonholes. The decorative buttons go through the front layer, and the inexpensive buttons go through the underlayer. When it's time for a wash, she just slips the button sets out of the garment altogether.

Peek-A-Boo Pants
DESIGNER
Sonia A. Huber

For an interesting flash of color and pattern, recycle men's neckties by inserting them into the side seams of pants or skirts.

MATERIALS AND SUPPLIES

- Pattern for pull-on pants

- Fabric of choice

- One or two men's ties to coordinate with pants fabric (the amount of "peek" will be determined by the tie's width)

- Notions required by pattern

CONSTRUCTION DETAILS

1. Cut pants pattern out of selected fabric. NOTE: The tie is inserted into the side seam before sewing the inseam closed.

2. Prepare tie(s) by cleaning, opening seams, and carefully removing interfacing and lining pieces. Press tie flat, taking care not to stretch the bias.

3. Fold tie in half, right sides together, and press lightly along fold. This pressed center mark will be important in a later step.

4. You will notice that the two edges of the wide end are asymmetrical; fold the tie in half and trim off the area shown in Figure 1, so points A and B are symmetrical.

5. Square off the wide end of the tie.

6. Fold the narrow end of the tie back on itself to the midsection. Trim the four edges even with one another to assure that less fabric will need to be fed into the waistline seam.

7. Stitch the tie to the front pants leg first, with wide end of the tie at the bottom edge, and stitching from hem to waist.

8. Stitch the tie to the back pants leg, keeping front free.

A RECYCLED NECKTIE MAKES A NICELY PATTERNED INSERTION PANEL FOR THESE SWISHY SILK PANTS. A SURPRISING PEEK-A-BOO FLASH OF THE TIE PANELS CREATES INTEREST WHEN SITTING OR DANCING.

9. Trim tie panel even with pants' top edge. Finish seams with serger or preferred method.

10. Press seams toward the pants legs, slightly favoring the pants fabric so tie panel won't show on the right side when standing still.

11. If desired, edgestitch closely along pressed edges.

12. To keep the tie panel from gaping open above the hipline, the pattern's side seam is sewn shut. Beginning at the waist edge on the wrong side, fold along the center tie marking and pin the pants side seams together, keeping the tie panel seams out of the way.

A MAN'S NECKTIE IS THE PERFECT SHAPE FOR A FLARED SIDE SEAM INSERTION OR PATTERNED PANEL INSIDE A SKIRT'S KICK PLEAT. THE TIE'S BIAS CUT HELPS IT TO MOVE GRACEFULLY WITH THE GARMENT IT IS STITCHED INTO.

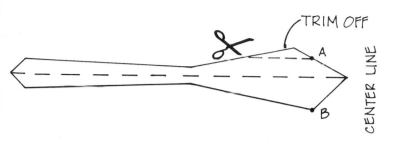

TRIM OFF

A

B

CENTER LINE

FIGURE 1

13. Stitch the pattern seamline from the top edge to about 12" (30.5 cm) below the waistline.

14. On the wrong side, press the tie flat and pants seam open only to the end of the stitching.

15. On the right side, butt the pressed edges of the pants fabric together; press the seams and the tie panel flat (you should not be able to see the tie panel).

16. With pants fabric edges still butted together, make several bar tacks at intervals of about 8" (20.5 cm), from the bottom of the side seam stitching to the lower edge. For a bit of extra flare, leave the hem edge open.

17. Complete pants according to pattern instructions.

Tips from the designer

■ Men's ties often come in beautiful patterns you never see in fabric by the yard, so they are a great source of interesting design accent. Incorporate a tie into any garment (skirt kick pleat, center back of shirt, jacket sleeve) simply by slashing the pattern piece where the tie panel is desired, remembering to add seam allowances to each slashed edge.

■ For an added touch, sew interesting buttons or beads on top of the bar tacks, or stitch small tabs into the seams that button across the peek-a-boo insertion.

PLAN FOR THE WEEK

Monday

Tuesday

Wednesday
Pretreat pants fabric.

Thursday
Lay out, cut, and mark pants; interface appropriate pieces.

Friday
Prepare tie for insertion; press center mark; trim ends even; square wide end.

Saturday
Stitch tie panel to pants legs; stitch original side seam to hip area; press.

Sunday
Make bar tacks across peek-a-boo seam; complete pants assembly.

Bandanna Prairie Skirt

DESIGNER

Joyce Baldwin

Turn a simple A-line skirt pattern into a lacy petticoat underneath boldly colorful bandanna panels, for an appealing country look.

MATERIALS AND SUPPLIES

■ Pattern for A-line skirt, preferably one with waist darts instead of gathers to reduce bulk

■ Fabric of choice for petticoat

■ Two large bandanna yardage panels or eight bandanna scarves. Panels shown here are finished size of 32½" (82.5 cm) square.

■ Eyelet lace with one finished edge, 4½-5" (11.5-12.5 cm) wide. If pre-gathered, purchase length equal to petticoat hem circumference plus extra for seam joining. If not gathered, purchase 2½-3 times petticoat hem circumference, depending on how tightly you intend to gather the eyelet ruffle.

■ Coordinating fabric or grosgrain ribbon for waistband

■ Notions required by pattern

CONSTRUCTION DETAILS

1. If using bandanna scarves, stitch together to form front and back panels. If using bandanna yardage, cut and hem front and back panels along sides and bottom.

2. Alter A-line skirt pattern so petticoat will be several inches longer than bandanna panels.

3. Assemble petticoat up to waistband attachment.

4. Gather upper edges of front and back bandanna panels to match front and back waist of petticoat; baste petticoat and panels together along waist.

5. Attach waistband, using preferred method.

6. Determine length of petticoat, so that eyelet lace will extend desired amount below bandanna panels; trim excess fabric. Hem petticoat.

7. If using ungathered eyelet lace, gather to match petticoat bottom edge. Attach eyelet ruffle to lower edge of petticoat.

Tips from the designer

■ When I saw these oversize scarf panels by the yard, the idea of a country-apron look popped into my head, but you could use any type of fabric panel to form an open-sided apron or closed-sided overskirt. Consider the alternatives, such as sheer silk scarves, contrasting eyelet fabric, or even nice dinner napkins. Just stitch smaller squares or rectangles together to get the panel size you want.

STORE-BOUGHT EYELET LACE MAKES A PRETTY AND QUICK RUFFLE THAT
PEEKS OUT FROM UNDER THE SCARF PANELS. TO SAVE EVEN MORE TIME,
PURCHASE PRE-GATHERED EYELET.

PLAN FOR THE WEEK

Monday

Tuesday

Wednesday
Pretreat fabrics.

Thursday
Hem bandanna yardage or stitch together bandanna scarves; modify skirt pattern as needed for length.

Friday
Lay out, cut, and mark petticoat fabric; interface appropriate pieces.

Saturday
Assemble petticoat; baste on bandanna panels; attach waistband.

Sunday
Determine petticoat length; hem petticoat; gather and attach eyelet ruffle.

Fringed Flair
DESIGNER
M. Luanne Carson

Take advantage of a cotton fabric's fringed selvage to create a touch of textural interest on an otherwise plain skirt style. Coordinate this casual look with a pretty flowered blouse.

DESIGN DETAILS

■ The designer added big apron-like patch pockets to this standard four-gore skirt style. She cut the pocket sides along the fringed selvage of the fabric and then stitched strips of selvage along the pocket bottoms for the fringed outline around two edges of each pocket.

■ For extra comfort, she elasticized the waistband with a non-roll type of elastic and stitched it in a single thickness for a low-bulk result.

Tips from the designer

■ Most of us just cut away the selvages of fabric and throw them away. But selvages can be interesting or pretty, so it pays to take a moment and study whether they can be put to attractive or efficient use. Fringe or pretty selvage patterns can add an interesting touch, and the fact that they require no further finishing saves sewing time.

CUTTING POCKETS ALONG THE FRINGED SELVAGE SAVES SEAM-FINISHING TIME AND ADDS A NICE TEXTURE TO A PLAIN FABRIC. EXTRA SELVAGE STRIPS STITCHED INTO THE SEAM ALONG THE POCKET BOTTOM MAKE IT LOOK AS THOUGH YOU SPENT HOURS FRINGING SQUARES OF FABRIC; ONLY YOU WILL KNOW IT WAS A SNAP.

Pat's Perfect Pajama Pants
DESIGNER
Pat Scheible

Use your basic slacks pattern to fashion variations like these no-side-seam casual pajama pants and harem pants that feel luscious and look great.

MATERIALS AND SUPPLIES

- Pattern for well-fitting slacks
- Fabric of choice
- Elastic, 1" (2.5 cm) wide
- Pattern tracing paper, brown wrapping paper, or newsprint

CONSTRUCTION DETAILS

1. Lay out front and back pattern pieces on tracing paper or alternative, making sure the crotch depth lines are aligned perfectly. See Figure 1.

2. Position pattern pieces so that the seamlines at the widest part of the hip are 1" (2.5 cm) apart. Weight pieces down.

3. Draw new inseam lines perpendicular to crotch depth lines.

4. Connect front and back waistlines. For a 1" (2.5 cm) elastic waistband, measure up from this line 2½" (6.5 cm). This is twice the width of the elastic, plus ½" (1.25 cm) seam allowance. Draw a line parallel to the first.

5. Connect front and back hem edges.

6. This is your new pattern. Cut out two pieces from the selected fabric, mark front and back, and assemble pants, using a serger and ¼" (6 mm) seam allowances.

7. Serge raw waist edge, turn to inside to form casing for elastic, press.

8. Open out casing and make a ½" (1.25 cm) buttonhole on each side of the center front, 1½" (4 cm) apart, through the front layer of the waistband. Turn casing back to inside and stitch around waistline.

CUT THE ANKLE BAND ON THIS HAREM PANTS VARIATION SO IT JUST SLIPS OVER YOUR FOOT. THE PANTS SHOULD BE LONG ENOUGH TO SKIM THE TOP OF THE FOOT, WITHOUT BUCKLING.

9. Cut a piece of elastic 2-3" (5-7.5 cm) shorter than your waist measurement.

10. Make simple self-fabric ties, about 12" (30.5 cm) long, by cutting along selvage and folding selvage over raw edge to stitch. See Figure 2. Attach ties to ends of elastic.

11. Insert tie through buttonhole and casing. Tie as desired.

12. Hem pants.

Harem Pants Variation

1. For the variation shown here, start with the Perfect Pajama Pants and shorten the hem edge as needed to just skim over the top of the foot, without buckling. The designer shortened hers by 4" (10 cm).

2. Gather the hem edge into a self-fabric or contrasting band that is cut long enough to just slip over the foot.

3. Use a slightly heavier weight fabric than the pajama pants for a crisper look, or use a drapey fabric and interface the ankle band enough to hold its shape.

■ This style of pants can be very baggy, so I prefer to start with the trim fit of a European slacks pattern. European patterns fit higher and closer in the crotch than American patterns, and they give a trimmer fit in the seat area.

■ For best results, these pants should be made out of a very lightweight, drapey fabric. I've used rayon crepe from the 1930s and black wool jersey for two different, but successful, looks.

■ Educate your fingers! Visit a fine fabric store and learn to identify fibers and judge quality by feel. You'll then be able to find the real gems among the unmarked bolts and remnants at fabric warehouses and discount shops. That's how I discovered the 1930s rayon crepe for these green pants.

■ It pays to invest in a dress form, to help fit your clothes to your unique figure. And when you're not sewing, you can use it to display a beautiful antique garment, a selection of scarves, or the fabric for your next project.

PLAN FOR THE WEEK

Monday

Tuesday

Wednesday

Thursday

Friday
Pretreat fabric.

Saturday
Draw new pattern; cut out pants; begin pants assembly.

Sunday
Make buttonholes in waistband; complete ties and casing; hem pants.

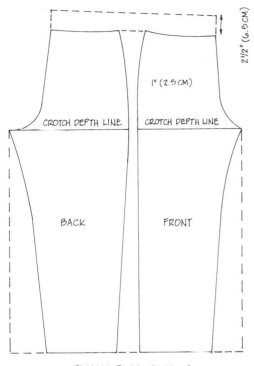

2½" (6.5CM)

1" (2.5CM)

CROTCH DEPTH LINE   CROTCH DEPTH LINE

BACK   FRONT

PAJAMA PANTS PATTERN

SELVAGE

MAKING A TIE

Complementary Angles
DESIGNER
M. Luanne Carson

The best way to find a perfect companion for this purchased sweater top with unusual angled design lines was to fashion this high-waisted model with angled insertion.

DESIGN AND CONSTRUCTION DETAILS

After purchasing this unusual, asymmetrical sweater fashion, the designer kept her eye out for a matching fabric and eventually found this perfect color companion in a cotton knit.

■ She varied a standard four-gore skirt style to go with the short sweater by adding a raised waistband and an asymmetrical waist-high insertion at the side. The insertion's angle contrasts nicely with the angle of the sweater hem.

■ To keep the waistband pulled up straight, she attached the skirt's top edge to a recycled silk undershirt that was shortened as needed. The undershirt keeps the skirt sitting correctly on the figure so its waistline doesn't pull down below the sweater's lower edge. It's also very comfortable to wear!

A SILK UNDERSHIRT WAS RECYCLED BY SHORTENING IT AND ATTACHING IT TO THE SKIRT WAISTBAND, TO PROVIDE SUPPORT AND KEEP THE HIGH WAIST SITTING CORRECTLY ON THE FIGURE WHEN WORN WITH THIS SHORT SWEATER.

Reversible Wrapper

DESIGNER
Marion E. Mathews

Turn any skirt into a reversible fashion with just a few easy adaptations, and get two garments for the time spent on one.

DESIGN AND CONSTRUCTION DETAILS

The designer chose a wrap-skirt pattern for a casual look, and then decided to make it reversible. For little additional time spent on the garment, she got two different-looking skirts.

■ She first stitched the skirt panels together out of each fabric and then sewed the two skirts to each other along the hem and wrap opening edges, with right sides together. After turning the double-layer skirt right side out, she topstitched along the wrap-front and hem edges to hold the layers together and provide a clean, finished look.

■ She then gathered the double-layer skirt onto the waistband and attached self-fabric ties at each side seam and wrap edge. No matter which side is worn out, one set of ties holds the skirt closed and the other set can be tucked inside.

■ On the solid blue side, she appliquéd a motif cut out of the print fabric to a patch pocket, to coordinate with the print fabric waistband.

Tips from the Designer

■ When making reversible garments, select compatible materials such as two sheers, two lightweight fabrics, or two fabrics that are equally crisp. A drapey rayon will not pair well with a stiff cotton. Be sure, also, that colors and patterns don't contrast so much that they show through to the other layer.

■ Sew small pieces of hook-and-loop tape inside the waistband to hold the skirt in place no matter which side shows: put the hook side of the tape on the print fabric of one wrap-front panel and the loop side on the solid fabric of the opposite panel.

■ Instead of ties at the wrap front, you could use a series of buttonholes and decorative buttons.

Turn a six-gore skirt into a graceful style with a combination of gathers and pleats. for a controlled and flattering drape.

THE INVERTED PLEATS MADE ON TOP OF THE GORE SEAMS ARE COMBINED WITH ELASTICIZED GATHERS TO CONTROL THIS SKIRT'S FULLNESS, BUT WITHOUT THE BULK OF A FULLY ELASTICIZED WAIST.

DESIGN AND CONSTRUCTION DETAILS

The designer started with a pattern she already had in her inventory for a six-gore, A-line skirt, but wanted a fuller, more fluid style to go with this beautiful, drapey fabric. She also made some other changes so the finished garment would suit her wearing preferences.

■ She added to the center front and back panels by placing the middle gore pattern piece 1½" (4 cm) in from the foldline before cutting. See Figure 1. This added 3" (7.5 cm) of extra width to both center panels.

■ Starting at the bottom of the side gore pattern pieces, she straightened the side edges up from the hem to the waist. See Figure 2. This eliminated the "A" line of the skirt and added width at the waist, which would later be drawn in by the gathers and inverted pleats.

■ She stitched the gores together and then created inverted pleats on the front and back gore seams. See Figure 3.

■ As a lover of convenient pockets, she also added inseam pockets.

■ She then cut a waistband to equal the pleated waistline size, attached it to the skirt, and finished it to make a casing. She cut a piece of elastic 3-4" (7.5-10 cm) smaller than her waist measurement, and then cut the elastic in half. She made slits in the waistband at the side seams on the inside, inserted one elastic piece into the skirt front and the other piece into the skirt back, distributing the gathers evenly between the inverted pleats. To encase the elastic ends inside the casing, she butted them together and zigzagged over the joint, using a scrap of seam binding as a foundation. See Figure 4. To hold everything in place, she stitched through all thicknesses at several points along the waistband.

■ As a finishing touch, she added belt carriers at the side seams and the front and back pleats.

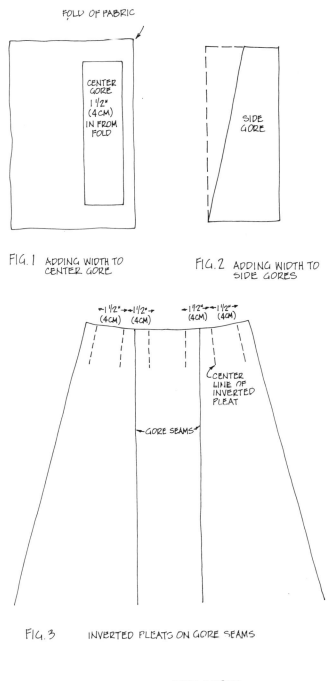

FIG. 1   ADDING WIDTH TO CENTER GORE

FIG. 2   ADDING WIDTH TO SIDE GORES

FIG. 3   INVERTED PLEATS ON GORE SEAMS

FIG. 4   SECURING ENDS OF ELASTIC

Tips from the designer

■ This combination of inverted pleats and elasticized gathers makes a really nice draped effect, without the considerable bulk of a fully elasticized waist.

■ Pockets are such a convenience, and it's easy to add them to a no-pocket pattern. Just use the pocket piece from another pattern, cut it out four times, and stitch the pocket pieces to the front and back side seams in a ⅜" (1 cm) seam allowance. Then, widen the front and back side seams just a little, stitch them from hem to waist, sewing around the pocket bag shape as you go.

■ I have found that inserting the waistband elastic in two half-sections makes it so much easier to pull the elastic all the way through the casing and distribute the gathers evenly.

PLAN FOR THE WEEK

Monday

Tuesday

Wednesday
Pretreat fabric.

Thursday
Make pattern modifications.

Friday
Lay out, cut, and mark skirt; interface appropriate pieces.

Saturday
Begin skirt assembly; cut waistband to fit; make belt carriers.

Sunday
Complete skirt assembly; attach waistband; insert elastic; attach belt carriers; hem skirt.

Classy Camouflage
DESIGNER
Becky Brodersen

These classy slacks eliminate a bulky fly front and replace it with a sleek and attractive angled front flap.

MATERIALS AND SUPPLIES

■ Pattern for pants with front pleats or darts and zipper front opening

■ Fabric of choice

■ Tissue paper or pattern tracing paper

■ Notions required by pattern

CONSTRUCTION DETAILS

1. Trim excess pattern tissue (beyond cutting lines) from top and center front of pants front pattern piece.

2. Pin pleats or darts closed, and fold toward side seam.

3. Tape a fresh piece of tissue or pattern tracing paper on top of the pants front pattern. Trace the center front line and the top edge of the pants pattern.

4. Measure 4" (10 cm) over from center front along the waist seamline and mark. See illustration.

5. Draw a line from this mark to the mark on the pattern where the crotch seam starts below the zipper (the mark is on the center front seamline). Add a ⅝" (1.5 cm) seam allowance to this line, pivoting opposite the mark on the pattern and continuing down about 1¼" (3 cm).

6. The extension for the front pattern piece is now complete. Trim the fresh tissue along the lines you drew and tape the extension to the pants front pattern piece along the center front line. If the pattern has pleats, check that the new extension will not cover the pleat nearest the center front; you may have to move the pleat over just a little.

7. To make a pattern for facings, trace the extension again. Draw a line 1" (2.5 cm) beyond the center front line to make the facing wide enough that it will cover well.

8. Cut out two pants front pieces, including the extension.

Mark center fronts on fabric. Cut two facing pieces.

9. Begin pants construction, following pattern instructions, through crotch seam step.

10. Finish facings along the straight center front edge, by serging or overcasting.

11. Sew facings to extensions, starting at the end of the crotch seam. Trim seam allowances and turn facings to inside. Press in place and baste along waistline edge.

12. On right side, topstitch each extension along angled edge, to a point about ½" (1.25 cm) before beginning of crotch seam. Overlap front extensions, pin in place, and topstitch from previous stopping point about 1-2" (2.5-5 cm) along crotch seam. This will hold the extensions in place inside the pants front.

13. Extend the waistband pattern to fit the new pants front by adding the same 4⅝" (11.75 cm) to each side of center front on the waistband, just as you did on the pants front pattern.

14. Attach waistband as usual, but baste it to the front extensions for a final fit before sewing in place. Hand sew hook-and-bar fasteners to inside of extensions.

Tips from the designer

■ Make sure you do a final fitting before the last bit of topstitching along the crotch seam, just in case you have to adjust anything. During this final fit, I also found that I had to pull the points of the front extensions into the waistband about ¼" (6 mm) to make sure everything would be smooth in the front.

SUBSTITUTING A ZIPPER FLY FRONT WITH THIS ANGLED EXTENSION IS EASY TO DO, CUTS DOWN ON BULK IN FRONT, AND LOOKS SMOOTH AND SLEEK. JUST TRACE THE FRONT PATTERN PIECE AND ADD THE EXTENSION, AND THEN EXTEND THE WAISTBAND THE SAME AMOUNT.

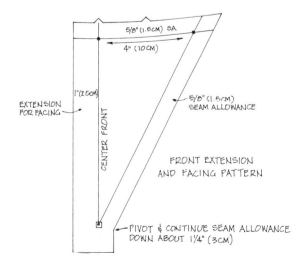

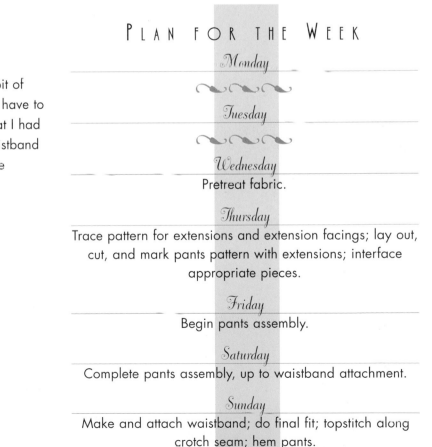

PLAN FOR THE WEEK

Monday

Tuesday

Wednesday
Pretreat fabric.

Thursday
Trace pattern for extensions and extension facings; lay out, cut, and mark pants pattern with extensions; interface appropriate pieces.

Friday
Begin pants assembly.

Saturday
Complete pants assembly, up to waistband attachment.

Sunday
Make and attach waistband; do final fit; topstitch along crotch seam; hem pants.

Faux Fur with Fringe

DESIGNER
Laurie Cervantes

Have some fun and change your image with this Dalmatian print faux fur miniskirt that sparks up a black sweater and tights.

MATERIALS AND SUPPLIES

■ Pattern for slim-fitting skirt with waist darts and no waistband

■ Fabric of choice, 1/2 yard (.5 m) remnant for miniskirt

■ Black fringe, 1 1/2" (4 cm) wide, 1 yard (.95 m) for short skirt plus 4 1/2" (11.5 cm) for pocket trim

■ Black piping or cord trim for pocket, 7" (18 cm) long

■ Zipper foot to stitch piping

■ Notions required by pattern

CONSTRUCTION DETAILS

1. Shorten pattern to above-knee length. Skirt shown is 15" (38 cm) long.

2. Make darts in front and back skirt sections according to pattern instructions. Stitch center back seam and insert zipper. Do not stitch front and back sections together yet.

3. For mock pocket, cut pieces as shown in Figure 1. Apply interfacing to wrong side, trimming 1/4" (6 mm) from sides and lower edge, and 1/2" (1.25 cm) from top edge.

4. Use a chalk mark to indicate center of piping and fringe. Stitch piping and fringe together, matching center points. Use a zipper foot to stitch as close to piping as possible.

5. Match center point of combined trim to point of pocket flap, and stitch trim to right side of pocket flap sides and lower edge, using a 1/4" (6 mm) seam allowance. See Figure 2. Piping should be next to right side of pocket flap, with fringe on top. Trim will not extend all the way to the top edge of the pocket flap, to minimize the bulk of piping in the seam.

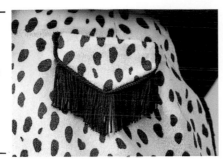

FRINGE ADDS MOVEMENT AND FUN TO THIS PARTY SKIRT. THE MOCK POCKET IS TRIMMED WITH THE FRINGE STITCHED TO BLACK PIPING, FOR A NICE DEFINED EDGE.

6. Press seam toward back of pocket flap, fringe and piping toward front.

7. Determine placement of pocket flap on skirt front as desired. Pocket placement on skirt shown here is 1½" (4 cm) below top edge of skirt and 2¼" (5.5 cm) left of center.

8. With right sides together and pocket flap upside down, stitch upper edge of pocket to skirt front, using ½" (1.25 cm) seam allowances. Press pocket flap down and tack in place.

9. Complete skirt construction, stitching fringe into side seams, or baste fringe to skirt front before sewing to skirt back. Press side seams open, with fringe seam allowance toward back.

■ Faux fur is frequently used for collars and cuffs, but I decided to use it for this festive skirt. The fringe adds movement and fun. Don't be afraid to experiment with wild or unusual fabrics and trims; purchase a few remnants and give it a try.

■ Faux fur requires a little special handling. The woven backing on this sample had a very firm finish; therefore, I lined the skirt for comfort and so the inside would skim over my tights or hose without catching. When pressing faux fur seams, use the lowest heat setting possible and very light steam; press on the wrong side only. Thicker fur piles may require finger-pressing only or the use of a needle board to prevent flattening the fibers. To reduce bulk in the seam allowances, you can shave the fibers off the backing.

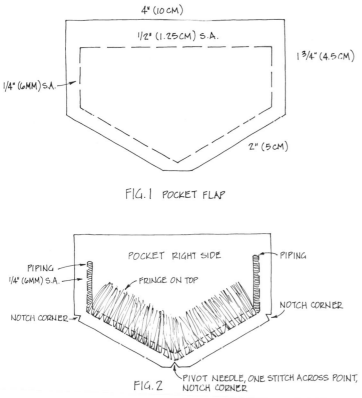

FIG. 1 POCKET FLAP

4" (10 CM)
1/2" (1.25 CM) S.A.
1 3/4" (4.5 CM)
1/4" (6MM) S.A.
2" (5 CM)

POCKET RIGHT SIDE
PIPING
1/4" (6MM) S.A.
FRINGE ON TOP
PIPING
NOTCH CORNER
NOTCH CORNER
FIG. 2
PIVOT NEEDLE, ONE STITCH ACROSS POINT, NOTCH CORNER

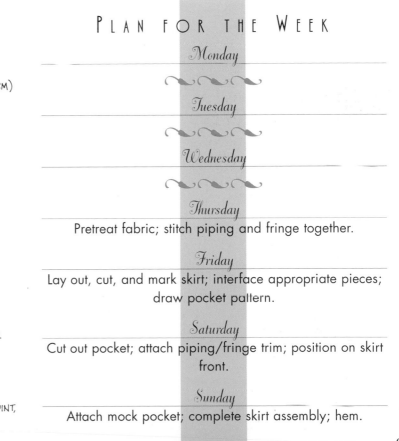

PLAN FOR THE WEEK

Monday

Tuesday

Wednesday

Thursday
Pretreat fabric; stitch piping and fringe together.

Friday
Lay out, cut, and mark skirt; interface appropriate pieces; draw pocket pattern.

Saturday
Cut out pocket; attach piping/fringe trim; position on skirt front.

Sunday
Attach mock pocket; complete skirt assembly; hem.

Swirls of Lace
DESIGNER
Elizabeth Searle

Add some lacy insertions to a simple gored skirt for a luscious, feminine flair that swishes seductively around the legs.

MATERIALS AND SUPPLIES

- Pattern for gored skirt (skirt shown here is four-gore)
- Fabric of choice
- Lace for insertions, approximately ½ yard (.5 m) for four godets
- Bridal hem binding
- Covered button kit
- Cardboard or other stiff paper
- Notions required by pattern

CONSTRUCTION DETAILS

1. Make a cardboard or paper wedge-shaped template for the triangular lace godets or insertions. See Figure 1. Be sure to add a seam allowance to all sides.

2. Cut out a godet for each gored seam (e.g., four godets for four-gore skirt, six godets for six-gore skirt). In the skirt shown here, the four godets are 18" (45.5 cm) tall.

3. Assemble skirt, following pattern instructions, leaving gored seams open the amount needed to accommodate godets.

4. Right sides together, pin godets into open seams, matching straight edges of godets with raw edges of skirt seams. Stitch each side of godet separately, from hem to point. Press godet seams toward skirt, and press skirt seams open above point of godet.

5. Complete skirt construction, following pattern instructions.

6. Stitch bridal hem binding to raw hem edge of skirt. Trim seam to a very narrow width. Turn hem binding to inside and hand stitch in place.

7. Cut circles out of skirt fabric and lace. Cover buttons with a circle of skirt fabric and a circle of lace on top. Hand sew or use hump-back safety pins to attach buttons at the point of each godet.

Tips from the designer

■ While it's so easy to add these lacy insertions to a gored skirt pattern, you can adapt any pattern. Just slash the skirt from hem to waist, to divide the skirt into gores, and add seam allowances to both slashed edges. Then, make godets of the desired size and fit them into the seams as above.

■ Bridal hem binding is lightweight and almost invisible, so it does not show through the lace at the hem. You can use strips of any tulle-like or net-like fabric for this purpose.

■ Instead of buttons to decorate the tops of the godets, use lace or fabric bows for a different look.

■ When covering buttons with a lacy or sheer fabric, always use a plain fabric underneath, so the metal won't show through.

PLAN FOR THE WEEK

Monday

Tuesday

Wednesday

Thursday
Pretreat fabrics; make template for godets.

Friday
Lay out, cut, and mark skirt; interface appropriate pieces.

Saturday
Begin skirt assembly; cut out and insert godets.

Sunday
Complete skirt assembly; hem skirt; cover and attach buttons.

THESE LACY GODETS INSERTED INTO THE SEAMS OF THIS FOUR-GORE SKIRT ADD FEMININE SWISH TO THE HEM. EACH ONE IS TOPPED OFF WITH A CUSTOM BUTTON COVERED WITH THE SKIRT FABRIC AND THEN THE LACE.

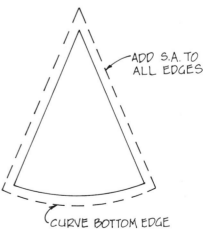

ADD S.A. TO ALL EDGES

CURVE BOTTOM EDGE

TEMPLATE FOR GODET.

FIG. 1

Parfait Swirl
DESIGNER
M. Luanne Carson

Adding a flouncy petticoat underneath a standard six-gore skirt makes this ensemble a study in swishy movement and rich dimension.

DESIGN AND CONSTRUCTION DETAILS

The designer started with a standard six-gore skirt pattern, which she coordinated with a separate jacket pattern. She altered and refined the skirt with these simple changes:

■ She added a lightweight cotton lawn petticoat underneath the skirt, for extra support but with a minimum of added bulk. The petticoat is made like a lining, attached to the skirt at the waist but hanging free at the sides and hem. It also acts as an underlining for the sheer skirt fabric so a separate slip doesn't have to be worn.

■ She trimmed the petticoat with a wide gathered self-fabric ruffle that just shows at the hem of the skirt. By attaching the ruffle to the petticoat layer instead of the skirt, the designer achieved a more sinuous, swirling effect. If the ruffle were attached to the skirt, it would have weighed the skirt down and the luscious swirling quality would have been lost.

■ She also elasticized the back half of the waistband, for wearing comfort and to echo the draped peplum-like ruffle on the back of the matching jacket.

Tips from the designer

■ The petticoat ruffle was cut on the straight grain, so it was easy to do a machine-rolled hem. However, the grain direction of the gored skirt varies along the hemline, making it difficult and exasperating to do a smooth rolled hem. Therefore, I used a sheer bias knit seam finish like Seams Great® to achieve a lightweight narrow hem. First, I stitched the sheer bias tape to the hem edge; the bias ensures that the tape will conform to the curved shape of the hem. Then, I turned it under and stitched close to the folded hem edge; the tape eliminated the need for any further seam finishing.

■ Don't forget to purchase some extra skirt fabric for the petticoat ruffle, especially if you want to gather it a lot, for a nice flounced effect. If you're using a wide fabric, rearrange the skirt cutting layout so you can cut the ruffle from the lengthwise edge.

■ Because portions of the skirt hem are on the slight bias, you may want to let the skirt hang overnight or up to a full 24 hours before hemming, so the various grainlines of the skirt can relax. However, you won't be able to notice a slightly uneven, undulating skirt hemline against the fluid petticoat ruffle on this fashion, so if you're strapped for time, don't bother with the overnight hanging and just make sure to hem the skirt high enough that it doesn't fall lower than the ruffle.

AN ELASTICIZED BACK WAISTBAND ON THE SKIRT COORDINATES WELL WITH THE DRAPED AND RUFFLED LOOK OF THE COORDINATING JACKET.

ATTACHING THE RUFFLE TO A SEPARATE PETTICOAT LAYER PROVIDES SUPPORT FOR THE SKIRT AND ACTS AS AN UNDERLINING FOR THE SHEER FABRIC. THE RESULT IS ALSO A MORE SENSUOUS AND FLUID LOOK THAN IF THE RUFFLE WERE SIMPLY SEWN TO THE BOTTOM EDGE OF THE SKIRT.

PLAN FOR THE WEEK

Monday

❧❧❧

Tuesday

❧❧❧

Wednesday
Pretreat fabrics.

Thursday
Lay out, cut, and mark skirt and petticoat fabrics; interface appropriate pieces; cut straight-grain petticoat ruffle from fashion fabric.

Friday
Assemble skirt up to waistband attachment.

Saturday
Assemble petticoat and attach ruffle; hem petticoat; baste skirt and petticoat together.

Sunday
Attach waistband; hem skirt to let desired amount of ruffle show underneath.

Sunrise Walking Shorts
DESIGNER
Joyce Baldwin

Do you hate to insert zippers or don't have one that matches the fabric? No problem...just change these side-zip walking shorts into a new look with a button opening

MATERIALS AND SUPPLIES

■ Pattern for walking or Bermuda shorts with side seam zipper

■ Fabric of choice, plus a little extra for button overlap, underlap, and facing

■ Tissue paper or pattern tracing paper

■ Notions required by pattern

CONSTRUCTION DETAILS

1. Measure diameter of selected buttons. The width of the button opening overlap and underlap must equal or slightly exceed button measurement.

2. Add overlap plus seam allowance to left front side seam pattern from waist to hem. See Figure 1.

3. Add underlap plus seam allowance to left back side seam pattern from waist to hem.

4. To make facing pattern for the left front button opening, lay tissue paper or pattern tracing paper over the altered seam. Trace new stitching and cutting lines, original stitching and cutting lines at waist, and original lower hem edge. The facing should be approximately 2½" (6.5 cm) wide as measured from the new stitching line of the side seam toward the center.

5. Make facing pattern as above for left back button opening.

6. Mark desired placement of buttonholes along left front button opening.

7. Alter waistband pattern to include overlap and underlap amounts.

8. Complete assembly according to pattern instructions, substituting faced button opening for stitched side seam with zipper.

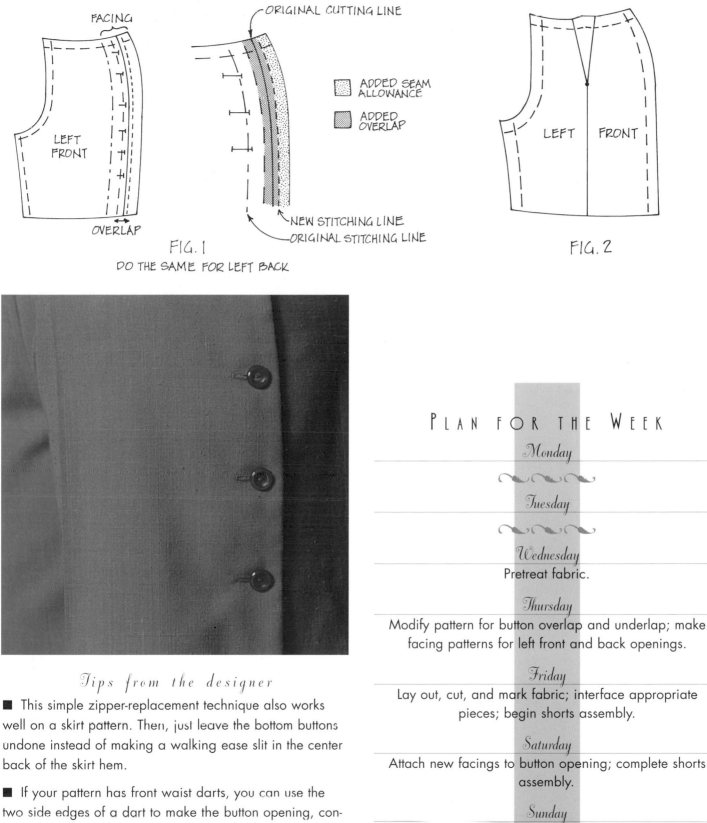

FACING

LEFT FRONT

OVERLAP

FIG. 1

DO THE SAME FOR LEFT BACK

ORIGINAL CUTTING LINE

ADDED SEAM ALLOWANCE

ADDED OVERLAP

NEW STITCHING LINE

ORIGINAL STITCHING LINE

LEFT | FRONT

FIG. 2

Tips from the designer

■ This simple zipper-replacement technique also works well on a skirt pattern. Then, just leave the bottom buttons undone instead of making a walking ease slit in the center back of the skirt hem.

■ If your pattern has front waist darts, you can use the two side edges of a dart to make the button opening, continuing down to the hem from the dart point. See Figure 2.

PLAN FOR THE WEEK

Monday

Tuesday

Wednesday
Pretreat fabric.

Thursday
Modify pattern for button overlap and underlap; make facing patterns for left front and back openings.

Friday
Lay out, cut, and mark fabric; interface appropriate pieces; begin shorts assembly.

Saturday
Attach new facings to button opening; complete shorts assembly.

Sunday
Attach waistband; make buttonholes and sew on buttons; hem shorts.

Wonderful Waistband
DESIGNER
Judith Robertson

Do something different and flatter your waist-line at the same time, with this wedge-shaped front waistband addition.

DESIGN DETAILS

The designer often completes a garment and then thinks, "This needs a little something else!" After finishing these walking shorts, she transformed the basic pattern into something special.

THIS ADDED FRONT EXTENSION MAY HAVE BEEN AN AFTERTHOUGHT, BUT IT SHOWS OFF A DECORATIVE BUTTON AND ADDS A NICE TOUCH OF FLAIR TO AN OTHERWISE PLAIN PATTERN.

■ To create the illusion of an asymmetrical belt, cover the fly front closure, and showcase a special button, she used leftover scraps to create a wedge-shaped front extension and tacked it right on top of the elasticized waistband at the side seam after the shorts were completed.

■ The added extension also flatters the waistline, because its asymmetrical angle breaks up the straight-across horizontal line. Such angles and asymmetrical style lines are always more slimming than straight lines, particularly horizontals.

■ The decorative button is just that—decorative. A simple hook-and-bar fastener holds the front extension in place, while the button adds just the right finishing touch.

■ Even though ethnic-type fabrics such as this don't require matching stripes or plaids, the designer spent just a little extra time aligning the linear motifs. The result is a neat, balanced look across the garment.

Custom Classic

DESIGNER
Marion E. Mathews

Turn a standard pattern into a custom garment just for you. by making simple changes according to your personal style preferences.

DESIGN AND CONSTRUCTION DETAILS

A lifetime of sewing experience has led the designer to form strong personal preferences about fit and look that don't always conform to standard pattern construction. For these customized pants, she started with a classic pattern with front and back waist pleats, slant pockets, and fly front. See Figure 1.

■ Believing that a fly-front opening and slant pockets are not very slimming, she moved the zipper opening to the center back seam and substituted inseam pockets at the sides. When cutting out the pants, she temporarily taped the front and side front pieces together along the original pocket slant line and cut them as one front piece. She allowed for slightly wider side seams on the pant legs, to ensure enough seam allowance to accommodate the inseam pockets. She then cut four pocket bag shapes from another pattern, two out of the pants fabric and two out of lining fabric.

■ To further reduce bulk at the side seams, she cut the self-fabric pocket bags and facings on the selvage so that no raw edges needed serging or turning under and finishing.

■ Due to natural figure changes over the years, the designer needs less curve in the back seat area of the pants. Therefore, she omitted the back waist pleats and, instead, evenly gathered the waistline onto the band. This released the back fullness from a higher point than pleats, and distributed it evenly across the entire back.

■ She eliminated the front waist pleats closest to the side seams and, instead, gathered the fullness onto the waistband. She kept the two centermost pleats, which align with the front crease line of the pants. The contrast between the

sleek and uncluttered center front and the gathered side fronts, along with the strong vertical line of the front pleats and crease, contributes to a very streamlined and slimming fashion.

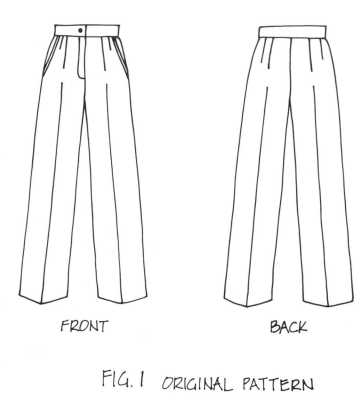

FRONT   BACK

FIG. 1 ORIGINAL PATTERN

Tips from the designer

■ One change that I make to all pants patterns is to add at least ½" (1.25 cm) to the standard 2" (5 cm) hem allowance. I find that the wider hem helps the pants hang better. In addition, the top of the hem on the inside of the pants leg won't be visible when you sit or cross your legs.

■ I almost always wear sweaters or jackets with pants, so moving the zipper to the back makes sense for me. The back location eliminates a bulky front opening and is hidden by other garments. It's also a lot faster to do than the more complicated fly front!

ABOVE: MOVING THE ZIPPER OPENING TO THE BACK OF THESE CLASSIC PANTS ELIMINATES THE BULK AND IS FASTER TO SEW THAN THE TRADITIONAL FLY FRONT. BELOW: THE DESIGNER REPLACED THE WAIST PLEATS WITH GATHERS ACROSS THE ENTIRE BACK, TO MORE EVENLY DISTRIBUTE FULLNESS AND DE-EMPHASIZE THE ORIGINAL PATTERN'S SEAT CURVE.

Eiffel Tower Suit
DESIGNER
M. Luanne Carson

A classic wool ensemble is streamlined with construction techniques that reduce bulk and then topped off with buttons reminiscent of the Eiffel Tower lit up at night.

DESIGN AND CONSTRUCTION DETAILS

Changes in the figure often show up first in the waist area, where we also like a lot of wearing comfort. Therefore, making pattern adaptations at the waist can turn a garment that's agonizing to wear into a wardrobe favorite. The designer made some adaptations to her standard six-gore skirt pattern to eliminate extra bulk, especially around the waist.

■ She made shaped buttonholes in the waistband and slipped a single thickness of a belt loop into each end. This eliminated the extra bulk of typical belt loops that are folded over and topstitched to the waistband. To make the buttonholes, she marked guidelines for a normal bound buttonhole and then freehand sketched the lozenge shape for the buttonhole opening. See Figure 1. The curved opening accommodates the thickness of the belt loop without stretching out of shape.

■ She contoured the waistband to match the curve of her figure, which is much more flattering and comfortable to wear than a straight-across waistband on a curved body. While the adaptation she made resulted in a raised waistband, a contoured version can also be made to fit lower, between the natural waistline and high hipline. See Figures 2-5 for making a custom contoured waistband.

Tips from the designer

■ A contoured waistband is so much more comfortable to wear. For a long-waisted figure, you can start your contoured waistband at the natural waistline and work up. For a short-waisted figure, you will want to start at the natural waistline and work down, by cutting away the desired width from the top of the skirt or pants and substituting the

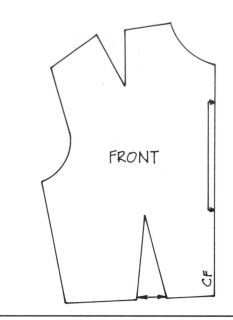

To reduce bulk at the waist and give a sleek effect, the ends of the belt loops were slipped into lozenge-shaped buttonholes instead of folded over and topstitched to the outside of the waistband.

Figure 2. To make a contoured waistband, start with a bodice pattern that fits you and fold the waist dart closed, as if you were going to stitch it. You will notice that the waist is now curved.

new lower waistband. Garments hang better from a contoured waist-after all, our bodies are curved, so shouldn't our clothes be curved as well?

■ If you don't have a custom sloper or master pattern fitted to your unique figure, you can purchase any pattern with a contoured waist and work from it. Regardless of the method you use, be sure to make a test waistband first because curving the upper and lower edges may result in a too-big or too-small waist circumference. To alter, slash through the upper or lower edge of the new waistband to, but not through, the opposite seamline, and spread apart or overlap to get an accurate waist fit.

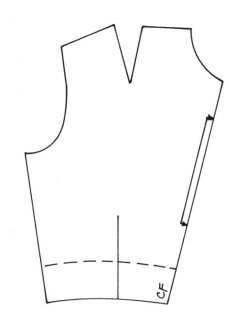

Figure 3. Trace the outline of the center front (or center back), waist edge, side edge, and a new curved line the desired distance from the waistline. This will indicate the finished width of the new waistband.

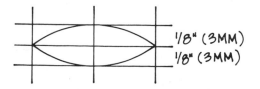

FIG. 1

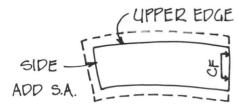

SIDE
ADD S.A.

UPPER EDGE

CF

FIGURE 4. ADD SEAM ALLOWANCES TO THE UPPER, SIDE, AND LOWER
EDGES IF YOU WILL BE CUTTING THE WAISTBAND ON THE FOLD. IF YOUR
GARMENT WILL HAVE A FRONT OR BACK OPENING, REMEMBER TO ADD A
SEAM ALLOWANCE AT THE CENTER FRONT OR CENTER BACK AND CUT OUT
TWO PIECES.

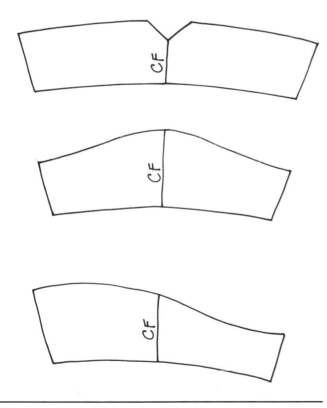

FIGURE 5. YOU CAN VARY THE SHAPE OF THE WAISTBAND FURTHER BY CRE-
ATING AN INDENTED WEDGE AT CENTER FRONT OR CENTER BACK (TOP),
EXAGGERATING THE CURVE OF THE WAISTBAND (CENTER), OR CREATING AN
ASYMMETRICAL SHAPE (BOTTOM).

A Well-Turned Leg

DESIGNER
Mary S. Parker

Spiff up the front of a new pair of casual pants with some Sashiko embroidery panels. It's a great way to showcase a new technique, and the interfaced embroidered panels protect the legs from the claws of a favorite cat purring in your lap.

MATERIALS AND SUPPLIES

■ Pattern for loose-fitting pants, preferably one that has pieced inset panels on the front legs (see Designer Tip below)

■ Tissue paper or pattern tracing paper, for modifying pants pattern without inset panels

■ Fabric of choice in a dark or bright color that will contrast with the white Sashiko embroidery thread, plus ¼ yard (.25 m) extra for adding seam allowances if modifying pattern without inset panels

■ ½ yard (.5 m) white cotton fusible interfacing

■ White topstitching weight thread

■ White regular weight thread

■ Iron-on transfer pens

■ Notions required by pattern

■ Sashiko designs of choice, available from various books on Sashiko embroidery. The flowers shown here were created by the designer to represent the cherry blossom and clematis.

CONSTRUCTION DETAILS

1. Cut pants pattern from selected fabric.

2. Cut fusible interfacing for inset panels that will be embroidered.

3. Enlarge selected Sashiko design to the size of the panel you will be embroidering, photocopy it, and draw over the design lines with iron-on transfer pens.

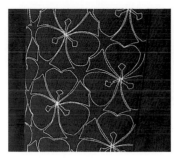

4. Fuse the interfacing to the wrong side of the inset panel, following manufacturer's directions.

5. Center the iron-on transfer design on the fused interfacing, ink side down. The right side of the fashion fabric will be face down on the ironing surface.

6. Iron the transfer design, according to manufacturer's directions, until the Sashiko design lines are transferred to the interfacing. Lift the transfer away and set aside.

7. Thread the sewing machine bobbin with topstitching weight thread and the needle with regular weight thread. You may have to loosen bobbin tension, as well as tighten needle tension, to make a good-looking stitch. Experiment on a fabric scrap before stitching on the garment pieces.

8. The Sashiko embroidery will be stitched with the right side of the fashion fabric against the feed dogs of the sewing machine, and the iron-on transfer design on top. Sew the design, following the iron-on transfer (see Designer Tip below).

9. Complete pants construction, according to pattern guide sheet.

Tips from the designer

■ To create the rectangular inset panels on an ordinary pants pattern, fold the pants front pattern piece in half and crease it, to identify the center front. Open up the pattern piece and draw two parallel lines approximately 4" (10 cm) on either side of the crease line. Cut the pattern piece apart along the parallel lines and then cut the resulting 8"-wide (20.5 cm-wide) center panel horizontally into rectangles. Add a standard seam allowance along the newly cut line of each piece. After completing the Sashiko embroidery on the desired panels, simply stitch the front pieces back together and proceed with pants construction.

■ It really helps to make some practice samples of the Sashiko embroidery, to get familiar with the stitching technique and check the tension settings of your machine. Working this out beforehand helps speed the embroidery stitching later!

■ Choose an embroidery design that can be stitched continuously from one edge of the inset panel to the other, so you don't have to stop and start, which results in thread tails that have to be tied off. Knots on the inside of the pant legs will not be comfortable against your skin! If your sewing machine has a needle-stop-down setting, it will be helpful to hold the fabric still when you pivot at turning points along the design lines.

■ For a special pair of gardener's pants, position the Sashiko panels further down the leg and stitch an extra layer of fabric inside the leg, leaving it open on top. You can insert a square of fleece, foam, or other padding for wonderful knee protection when weeding or digging in the garden. Then, just pull out the padding when the pants need to be washed.

PLAN FOR THE WEEK

Monday

Tuesday

Wednesday
Pretreat fabric.

Thursday
Modify pants pattern if necessary; make practice samples of Sashiko embroidery.

Friday
Lay out, cut, and mark pants; interface appropriate pieces; make Sashiko transfer design.

Saturday
Transfer iron-on Sashiko design; complete Sashiko embroidery.

Sunday
Complete pants assembly.

Evening Elegance
DESIGNER
M. Luanne Carson

Contrasting the matte and shiny sides of crepe-back satin fabric creates an interesting and classy look for evening pants. The unexpected sheen at the hemline is a nice surprise.

DESIGN DETAILS

■ The designer took advantage of the fabric's natural characteristics to slenderize her figure. The matte finish of the fabric's crepe side accentuates the muted color and vertical silhouette of the fluid pants style, which is naturally slimming. She then added two cuff tiers at the hem, with the shiny satin side on the outside. The reflective contrast suggests classic tuxedo trim and dresses up a very simple pattern. The sheen at the hem also draws attention to pretty feet in extra special shoes.

■ Crepe-back satin drapes beautifully and has a nice weight to it. The cuffs or folds of fabric add extra heft to the pant legs, for a romantic fluid look that hangs attractively on the figure.

THE SHINY SIDE OF CREPE-BACK SATIN ADDS A DRESSY LUSTER TO A SIMPLE PANT LEG AND CONTRASTS WITH THE CREPE SIDE FOR AN INTERESTING TWIST.

Draped for Effect
DESIGNER
Judith Robertson

An attached front drape creates the illusion of a wrap-style sarong skirt. and its pleated point is tacked down for a distinctive decorative effect.

DESIGN DETAILS

The designer often stitches up standard patterns and then concludes that they "need a little something else." In this case, she started with a basic gathered skirt and made a few changes.

■ Instead of gathering in the fullness of the skirt, she pleated it into a waistband, folding the pleats toward the center to create inverted box pleats at center front and back and two additional pleats on either side.

■ For the decorative front drape, she cut a triangle of self-fabric, finished the outer raw edges, folded over the top edge and stitched part of it in the ditch of the waist seam. She then pleated the free-hanging pointed end of the drape and tacked the pleats to the skirt front, to create the illusion of a wrapped and tied sarong.

A SINGLE THICKNESS OF SELF-FABRIC IS CUT TO FORM A DECORATIVE FRONT DRAPE, WHICH IS STITCHED PARTWAY INTO THE WAISTLINE SEAM. THE POINTED END IS LEFT HANGING FREE, THEN PLEATED AND TACKED TO THE SKIRT FRONT TO CREATE THE LOOK OF A KNOTTED SARONG STYLE.

Weekend Jumpsuit

DESIGNER
Piper Hubbell Robinson

This casual jumpsuit was made for style, comfort, and fun, but it also cleverly disguises figure challenges.

MATERIALS AND SUPPLIES

- Pattern for jumpsuit
- Coordinating fabrics of choice
- Twill tape or nylon stabilizing tape
- Custom belt components
- Notions required by pattern

DESIGN DETAILS

The designer describes her approach to this garment: "When one is short-legged and wider in the hips, pant styles should be chosen to not attract attention to this area. I try to achieve good fit and classic design in a dark or neutral color. When creating this project, I had to determine how to incorporate these requirements into an interesting design. That's why I decided on the jumpsuit."

- The lower part of the jumpsuit is neutral in color and simple in shape. The designer added visual length to the garment by creating a contrasting bodice 3" (7.5 cm) above the waistline. Most of the design interest is above the waistline, which both guides the observing eye upward and lengthens the appearance of the legs.

- The designer also made a surprising change that is not usual when de-emphasizing hips, thighs, and short leg length. She added patch pockets to that crucial area and made them baggy by cutting them wider at the top edge than the space allotted on the pant leg. The bagginess and darker color of the pocket hide the outline of the thigh.

- She finished the neckline and armhole edges with bias self-fabric strips sandwiched between the garment and facing strips sewn to the inside. This created a nice dimensional quality and an interesting diagonal stripe effect.

CONSTRUCTION DETAILS

1. Do a fitting of the selected jumpsuit pattern before making any changes, to check the fit of the crotch length.

2. Measure up 3" (7.5 cm) from the waistline and slash across the pattern piece, to create a horizontal seamline. Remember to add seam allowances to both slashed edges.

3. Mark the location of pockets, placing them mostly at the front of the leg rather than toward the hip. The pockets shown here were made to fit a rectangle measuring 11" by 16" (28 by 40.5 cm). The pockets themselves were cut 11" (28 cm) at the bottom edge, graduating out to 17" (43 cm) at the top edge, and 16" (40.5 cm) tall. The pockets were sewn to the pants legs to conform to an 11" (28 cm) width all the way up, forcing the wider top edges to bag out.

4. Make four belt carriers as long as required to extend from the top pocket edge into the bodice seam, and as wide as desired; those shown here are 3½" (9 cm) long and a finished width of ¾" (2 cm).

5. Catch the top ends of the carriers into the bodice seamline and stitch the bottom ends at the corner of each pocket.

6. To finish the neckline and armholes, stabilize these areas first by basting twill tape or nylon stabilizing tape along the seamline.

7. Make two sets of self-fabric bias strips (see page 28) to fit the neckline and armholes, one for the bias edging and the other for the facings. The strips shown here were cut 2" (5 cm) wide.

8. Fold one set of bias strips in half and baste to the right side of the neckline and armholes, matching raw edges.

9. Stitch other (unfolded) set of bias facing strips to garment edges, right sides together, sandwiching the folded bias strips in between. See Figure 1.

10. Trim seams, turn facing strips to inside and press. Turn under raw edge of facing strips and hand or machine sew to inside of garment.

11. Make matching or contrasting belt, as desired.

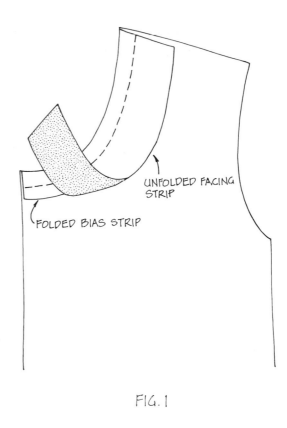

UNFOLDED FACING STRIP

FOLDED BIAS STRIP

FIG. 1

THE POCKETS WERE CUT WIDER AT THE TOP EDGE THAN THE BOTTOM AND ALONG THE FABRIC SELVAGE, TO CREATE A NICELY FRINGED EDGE AND A BAGGY QUALITY THAT DISGUISES THE THIGH SHAPE.

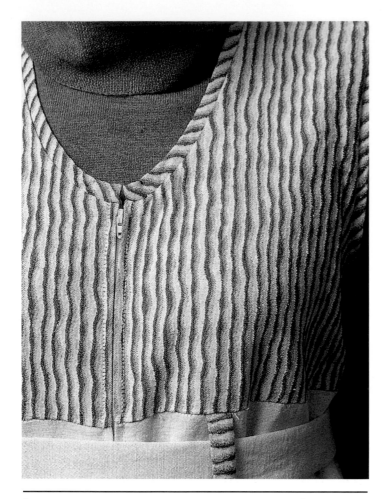

FOLDED SELF-FABRIC BIAS STRIPS WERE SANDWICHED BETWEEN THE GARMENT AND SELF-FABRIC FACING STRIPS FOR A CLEAN FINISH WITH AN ATTRACTIVE DIMENSIONAL QUALITY.

■ Keep your eyes out for interesting ways to use fabric selvages. By cutting out the pockets along the selvage, I ended up with a subtle fringe accent that would have been difficult to create any other way.

■ If you can't distinguish between the right and wrong side of a fabric, and if both sides are attractive, use them both for creative contrast. The bodice and pocket fabrics in this jumpsuit are the same, but one side is slightly darker than the other and provides a subtle color difference. I used the darker side for the pockets, to downplay the hip area.

Tips from the designer

■ The long belt carriers add one more vertical element to the jumpsuit and also create the illusion of more space between the upper and lower parts of the body. I made sure to match the belt color to the pants area, so it wouldn't be such a noticeable horizontal line, which might widen that area of the body. Instead of using a belt, you could thread a silky scarf through the loops or make a custom braid of the three fabrics (plain, right side of contrast fabric, wrong side of contrast fabric).

PLAN FOR THE WEEK

Monday

Tuesday

Wednesday

Thursday
Pretreat fabrics.

Friday
Lay out, cut, and mark jumpsuit pattern; interface appropriate pieces.

Saturday
Begin jumpsuit assembly; make belt carriers and baste in place; cut out and attach pockets.

Sunday
Complete jumpsuit assembly; finish neckline and armhole edges; make belt.

A Classic Redefined
DESIGNER
M. Luanne Carson

A classic trouser pattern takes on new elegance with vertical style lines added to lengthen and slim the figure.

DESIGN AND CONSTRUCTION DETAILS

The designer started with a classic trouser pattern that had darts in both front and back. She pieced a slimming vertical panel at the side front, replaced the back darts with vertical seams, and used the front darts to coordinate with the design of a custom design belt.

■ The added side front panel creates an additional vertical style line to slim the figure. The designer created a new seam by slashing the pants front pattern 3" (7.5 cm) in from the side seam, from waist to hem, and adding seam allowances. In addition to the original side seam, there is now a new vertical seam running up the leg and slightly off center; this draws the observing eye in from the hipline and up and down the figure, to add height and narrow the silhouette.

■ On the back pant pattern, she slashed the pattern from waist to hem, along a line right up the middle of the dart. She then stitched a narrow seam that lined up with the original dart legs (see Figure 1) and eased the little bit of extra fabric at the waist into the waistband. The back of the pants hang smoothly from the waist, with a vertical style line that visually breaks up side-to-side width and also adds length.

■ She made a custom belt out of coordinating fabrics and arranged it around the waistline until she got a sculpted effect that she liked. The belt's two downward points align with the front darts and further enhance the vertical effect of the overall look.

By aligning the points of the custom belt with the darted pleats in the front, the designer created an accessory that perfectly coordinates with the style lines of the garment. Simple details like this turn ordinary patterns into extraordinary fashions.

The designer slashed the back pant pattern from waist to hem, right down the middle of the dart. She then stitched a narrow seam that lined up with the original dart legs, to create these smooth, slimming vertical seams.

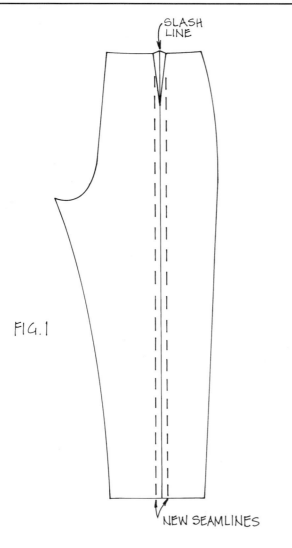

SLASH LINE

FIG. 1

NEW SEAMLINES

Tips from the designer

■ You can slash pattern pieces just about anywhere and add seam allowances, to create interesting style lines in a garment. It's easiest to slash along the straight of grain and make straight seams, but you can also curve and shape new seams for dramatic effect.

■ When making your own coordinating accessories, think about how you can echo the design lines of the garment. I play around with fabrics, trims, and shapes until I see something that just might work. It's definitely a very creative trial-and-error process, but I always come up with something great that I probably couldn't have planned in advance and certainly would never find in a store.

■ Belts are the perfect accessory for pants and skirts, and they can be unique expressions of your creativity. Don't settle for a boring leather belt with buckle when you can quickly make something special. You can braid cords or fabric strips together, twist store-bought braids into a rope, or piece strips of fabric or leather into interesting arrangements.

Too-Easy Wrap Skirt
DESIGNER
Pat Scheible

If you need a new skirt in a jiffy, here's a no-fail wrap style that is so easy and fast. Great for beginners or sewers who are short on time, because the pattern is simply a square.

MATERIALS AND SUPPLIES

■ Fabric of choice, preferably a non-clingy fabric with drape (see yardage requirements below)

■ Lightweight coordinating fabric or lining fabric for waistband facing

FABRIC REQUIREMENTS

■ Width required is hip measurement plus 2" (5 cm) ease, plus 8" (20.5 cm) or more as desired for overlap, plus 1½" (4 cm) hem for overlap, plus ¼" (6 mm) narrow hem for underlap.

■ Length required is desired skirt length, plus 1½" (4 cm) waistband, plus 1½" (4 cm) hem.

CONSTRUCTION DETAILS

1. Cut a square or rectangle of fabric to the width and length measurements you determined above. Serge all edges.

2. Make a ¼" (6 mm) narrow hem on the underlap edge, and topstitch in place.

3. Make a 1½" (4 cm) hem on the overlap edge and around the bottom edge. Miter corner (see Figure 1) and topstitch in place.

4. Wrap skirt with overlap on outside, and pin together so waist equals hip measurement plus 2" (5 cm). Stitch overlap along waist seamline.

5. Trim underlap close to seamline. See Figure 2.

6. Cut a waistband facing equal to your hip measurement. Stitch to right side of waistband, trim, and turn to inside to form casing for elastic. Stitch in the ditch of the previous seam, leaving an opening to insert elastic.

7. Topstitch top edge of waistband.

8. Insert elastic and slip stitch opening closed.

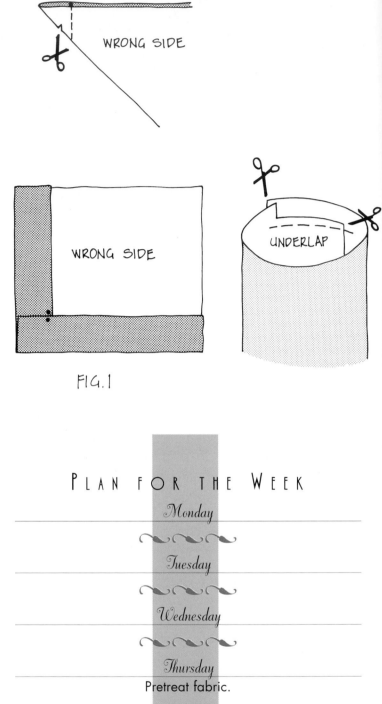

FIG. 1

Tips from the designer

■ Be sure to make your length measurements along the lengthwise grain of the fabric, so the finished skirt will hang correctly and not stretch out of shape. It really does matter which way the grain runs! Just remember: up and down for this and all skirts.

PLAN FOR THE WEEK

Monday

Tuesday

Wednesday

Thursday
Pretreat fabric.

Friday
Determine required yardage measurements; cut fabric rectangle; serge edges.

Saturday
Make hems; wrap and stitch skirt.

Sunday
Make waistband casing; insert elastic.

Skirt Revival

DESIGNER
Sallie Rae Ruff

Do you have a favorite old pattern but not enough fabric to make it? No problem...just apply a little creative ingenuity.

MATERIALS AND SUPPLIES

■ Pattern for basic gathered skirt

■ Assorted coordinating fabrics, including ¼ yard (.25 m) each for waistband and buttoned side bands

■ Notions required by pattern

DESIGN AND CONSTRUCTION DETAILS

The designer's favorite pattern called for 3 yards (2.75 m) of fabric, but she had only 2 yards (1.85 m) for the main part of the skirt. So she pulled out the pattern guide sheet to see what adjustments could be made and decided to create a contrasting button band down the side and a contrasting waistband. She got the most mileage possible out of limited fabrics and created some interest at the same time this way:

■ She cut long narrow strips of the black waistband fabric, folded them in half, pressed them, and then stitched them into the long button band seams. The result is a unifying transition between the main fabric and contrasting band fabric, as well as a nice outline of the button band.

■ She pieced together assorted scraps of the contrasting fabric to achieve the length needed for the side button band; for an interesting accent, she stitched narrow strips of main fabric into the joining seams.

■ She appliquéd rectangular scraps of the main fabric to the waistband before inserting the elastic, to create the illusion of a faux front belt and to soften the contrast between the skirt fabric and the black waistband.

Tips from the designer

■ This is one of my favorite patterns for a simple gathered skirt, and it is about ten years old. Instead of buying new patterns, I just adapt this one depending on the effect I've got in mind or the amount of fabric I have on hand. If you study the pattern instructions before cutting into your fabric, you can come up with all sorts of ideas for creative variation or problem-solving.

NARROW STRIPS OF CONTRASTING FABRIC STITCHED INTO THE BUTTON BAND SIDE SEAMS AND PIECING JOINTS CREATE COLORFUL INTEREST, AS WELL AS A NICE TRANSITION BETWEEN THE MAIN SKIRT FABRIC AND BUTTON BAND FABRIC.

PLAN FOR THE WEEK

Monday

Tuesday

Wednesday

Thursday
Pretreat fabric; make pattern modifications.

Friday
Lay out, cut, and mark skirt; interface appropriate pieces.

Saturday
Piece button band strips; begin skirt assembly.

Sunday
Complete skirt assembly; attach appliqué patches to waistband; attach waistband; hem skirt.

No-Sew Style

DESIGN DETAILS

Wrapping and typing a pareo or sarong in varying fashions is one of the quickest and easiest ways to create different looks. Start with a large fabric rectangle; the one shown here is 45" (1.1 m) wide and 2⅜ yards (2.2 m) long. Then, just follow the photographs and instructions below.

START WITH ONE CORNER AT THE HIP (LEFT), WRAP THE REMAINING FABRIC ALL THE WAY AROUND THE WAIST AND TIE TOGETHER AT THE HIP (CENTER). THE FINISHED LOOK (RIGHT) IS A TRADITIONAL SARONG STYLE.

FOLD ONE END OF THE FABRIC TO FORM A TRIANGLE (LEFT). PLACE THE POINT AT THE HIP, WRAP THE FABRIC AROUND THE WAIST AND TIE TO THE POINT OF THE TRIANGLE (CENTER). WRAP THE REMAINING LENGTH OF FABRIC AROUND THE WAIST AND TUCK IN TO FORM AN OVERLAP IN THE BACK (RIGHT).

Start with a rectangle of beautiful fabric and fashion several pants and skirt
styles without sewing a single stitch.

*Traditional
Sarong
Wrap*

*Triangle
Wrap*

Island Wrap (above)

START WITH ONE CORNER AT THE HIP (LEFT), WRAP THE REMAINING FABRIC ALL THE WAY AROUND THE WAIST AND TIE TOGETHER AT THE HIP, AS IN THE TRADITIONAL SARONG. FOLD THE REMAINING FABRIC BACK ON ITSELF (CENTER), AND TUCK IN AT THE WAIST (RIGHT).

Rice Paddy Wrap (below)

WRAP AND TIE BOTH CORNERS OF A SHORT END OF THE FABRIC AROUND THE WAIST (LEFT). PASS THE OPPOSITE SHORT END THROUGH THE LEGS AND TIE AROUND THE WAIST IN BACK (CENTER). THE FINISHED LOOK (RIGHT) IS COMFORTABLE AND QUICK.

ABOUT THE DESIGNERS

Joyce Baldwin

is Assistant Professor of Textiles at Western Carolina University in Cullowhee, North Carolina. She passes on her love of fabrics and fashion design to classrooms full of students, and plans annual student trips to the New York City fashion centers, where she also manages to shop for sewing supplies for her own studio.

Sheila Bennitt

recently relocated to Asheville, North Carolina from Texas, where she sold fanciful fashions from her design studio. She is also a painter and sees many parallels in design and technique between working with fabric and paint.

Becky Brodersen

enjoys sewing and learning about fiber arts and crafts. She lives in Nashville, Tennessee with her husband and three dogs.

M. Luanne Carson

thrives on the creative process of integrating fabric and style for unusual effect. She combines her formal training in clothing and textiles with her success as an educator to excite her students about their creative potential. Even after many years at the machine, sewing continues to galvanize Luanne's thoughts and activities. She lives in Arden, North Carolina.

Laurie Cervantes

has long enjoyed creating wearables and gifts for herself and others. She says that designing and constructing is a very satisfying and creative "workout." Laurie currently enjoys collecting vintage patterns and making them up in new fabrics. She lives in La Jolla, California.

Sally Hickerson

is the hospitable owner of Waechter's Silk Shop in Asheville, North Carolina, a favorite destination for fabric lovers. She also is an expert manager of her time, because she gets a lot of sewing done. Sally is a specialist in customizing patterns for her petite figure and adding flair to everything she makes.

Sonia A. Huber

says that taking classes in pattern drafting, after many years of sewing, opened up a new world for her. She has found that time is short for everyone, so she's learned to make simple changes to a favorite pattern. Sonia lives in Austin, TX.

Lisa Mandle

is the owner and principal designer of Only One, a custom one-of-a-kind clothing and accessories business in Marshall, North Carolina. She has had extensive experience in the fashion and costume design fields, and was selected in 1984 as one of the top ten designers in Washington, D.C. In her current business, she emphasizes the unique qualities of clothing and never makes a design from the collection the same way twice, hence the name, Only One.

Marion E. Mathews

of Asheville, North Carolina, got hooked on sewing when her grandmother let her use the old treadle machine. Since then, she has made her own wedding dress, children's clothes, men's sport coats, and much more. Although Marion soon switched from the treadle machine to a motorized version, she passed on her love of sewing and fabric to her daughter, the author.

Mary S. Parker

is descended from a long line of quilters and seamstresses. Her love of sewing and a fondness for cats have remained constant throughout a changing array of professional career positions. Mary lives in Asheville, North Carolina, and recently moved into a larger house with her understanding husband so that she would have sufficient room for her growing fabric stash.

Judith Robertson

has been sewing since she was 8 years old, and loves the challenge of making something that is distinctly her own. Because she is not too keen on frequent shopping, she enjoys using things that are already on hand, such as scraps of fabric, to add a twist to simple, time-tested designs. Judith lives in Asheville, NC.

Piper Hubbell Robinson

operates a one-of-a-kind garment design studio called Wear For Art Thou in Elmhurst, Illinois. She draws on her many years of classical ballet and her formal training in fashion design to interpret line, shape, form, and movement in fabric. Piper says the process of creating garments is completed by the act of wearing them.

Sallie Rae Ruff

started sewing when she was 12 years old. With an Associate Arts degree in Fashion Merchandising, Sallie has always dreamed of becoming a designer. She loves machine appliqué and uses it to give her custom "contemporary country" garments an individual touch. She lives in Cayce, SC.

Joneen M. Sargent

likes the creative outlet that sewing provides and loves to try new things. She started sewing back in high school and makes quilts and clothing for herself and her family. Joneen lives in Bristol, Tennessee.

Pat Scheible

is a decorative painter by trade. She designs and creates with fiber, paint, and most any other material that strikes her fancy. Pat lives in Mebane, North Carolina.

Elizabeth Searle

started sewing in the crib, according to her grandmother. She has a dressmaking business in Asheville, North Carolina, teaches creative sewing techniques in area classes, and still has time to experiment with creative art-to-wear clothing for herself and her clients.

ACKNOWLEDGMENTS

The behind-the-scenes support system of designers, photographers, models, friends, and others is indispensable to every author. No book would get done without these creative and generous folks, and my sincere thanks go to all of them:

- the designers, whose creativity, ingenuity, and sewing energy are truly inspiring.

- the models, who took time away from their real life occupations to dress up for an hour or so, and whose beauty and good humor brought the garments to life: Elizabeth Benischek, Sheila Bennitt, Naomi Brown, Beth Carter, Evans Carter, Jessi Cinque, Rachel Dial, Lisa Mandle, Lois Marsh, Gwendolyn Marvels, and Catharine Sutherland.

- photographers Richard Babb and Evan Bracken, who so graciously made themselves available at the last moment.

- the generous folks who lent furniture and accessories to use as photo props: Linda Constable at Sluder Furniture, Ronnie Myers at Magnolia Beauregard's Antiques, Craig Culbertson and Otto Hauser at Stuf Antiques, and Katie Skinner and Vann Boyd at the Loft, all of Asheville, North Carolina.

- Catharine Sutherland, for researching the history of the zipper, and Joyce Baldwin, for providing a treasure trove of historical information about the zipper.

- M. Luanne Carson, for the ingenious pocket designs on pages 64, 65.

- Dana Irwin, talented art director for the Weekend Sewer's series, fellow lover of textiles, owner of an amazing collection of accessories to put with the garments, and a great book production partner.

OUTTAKES

In the spirit of dressing up, we decided to share a few of the outtake photographs with you.

A-line. Skirt shape that is fitted at the waist and extends outward in a gentle angle to the hem.

accordion pleats. Very narrow pleats, narrower at the top than the bottom so they fan out at the bottom of the pleated area and form a zigzag edge. Also called sunray and fan pleats. See page 52.

baggies. Casual pants popular in the 1970s that are full through the hips, with legs that narrow at the ankles.

balloon shorts. Roomy shorts pleated into the waistband and gathered into bands at the hem.

balloon skirt. Skirt style that is gathered or pleated into the waistband and narrower at the hem. Similar to the hobble skirt and tulip skirt.

beach trousers. Long wide-legged pants popular in the 1920s and 1930s for wearing over swimming suits. Sometimes called beach pajamas.

bell bottoms. Pants that are fitted at the hip and flare out widely at the hem. Worn by sailors and by young people in the 1960s and 1970s. Sometimes called flares.

bellows pocket. Exterior pocket that expands out from the surface of the garment by means of an inverted pleat. Commonly seen on safari-type garments. See page 70.

Bermuda shorts. Shorts that reach almost to the knee. Popularized during the 1930s and 1940s at resort locations in Bermuda. Also called walking shorts.

bias. A fabric's diagonal direction. True bias is on a 45-degree diagonal across the straight grain. See page 28 for a discussion of bias.

bias cut. A garment cut on the bias, resulting in a drapey, figure-hugging silhouette.

bloomers. Loose, full-leg pants that are gathered at the ankles. Named for Amelia Jenks Bloomer (see page 33).

blue jeans. Casual fitted pants made of indigo-dyed denim and characterized by contrast top-stitching over flat-fell seams and copper rivets at stress points. Originated by Levi Strauss (see page 36). Also called denims.

boilersuit. All-in-one work garment that zips or buttons up the front and has long sleeves. Also called a jumpsuit.

box pleat. Pleat formed from two pleats facing in opposite directions. See page 52.

break. Point where the trouser crease is disrupted or "broken" by the hem hitting the top of the shoe.

broomstick skirt. Full skirt that is wrapped tightly around a broomstick after washing and while still wet, to form a crinkled appearance when dry.

cargo pocket. Large exterior pocket on pants or shorts that extends up and over the waistband to form a wide belt carrier.

casing. A passage formed by a facing or by folding down and stitching a fabric edge so a drawstring or elastic band can be threaded through.

Capri pants. A popular pants style in the 1950s, named after the Italian resort of Capri, that were tapered to above-ankle length, and slit at the side seam.

cartridge pleats. Small tubular pleats inspired by loops for bullets on military cartridge belts. See page 52.

circle skirt. Very full skirt made from a fabric circle or two half-circles stitched together. Popular in the 1950s. See page 13.

Clamdiggers. Mid-calf casual pants popular in the 1950s.

cluster pleats. Narrow pleats arranged in groups instead of distributed evenly across the fabric. See page 52.

color blocking. Use of large areas of contrasting colors in a garment to create graphic interest.

crotch. Location on pants where the legs meet, where the inseams intersect with the pants front and back. Sometimes called crutch.

crystal pleats. Permanent, heat-set pleats that are very narrow in width.

cuff. Folded-back band at hem of pants leg.

culottes. Divided skirt that forms casual, wide-legged pants.

dart. V-shaped tuck that shapes garment section to body contours.

denim. Twill-woven heavy-duty fabric used to make blue jeans. Named after Nîmes, France, where the fabric came from (serge de Nîmes). See blue jeans.

dirndl. Full skirt style that is gathered into the waistband. Also called peasant skirt.

drainpipes. Tight, narrow-leg pants popular in the 1960s. Also called stovepipes.

ease. Fullness of a garment above and beyond body measurements. Wearing ease is the minimum fullness required for mobility and comfort.

Design ease is the additional fullness over and above wearing ease that creates the distinctive look the designer intended.

easing. Matching the edges of two fabrics of different lengths, as in easing a sleeve into a slightly smaller armhole.

facing. Piece of self-fabric sewn to right or wrong side to finish a garment's raw edge, as in neckline, armhole, and sleeve facing.

fan pleats. See accordion pleats.

flares. Pants that are straight to the knee or below, and then quickly widen. Also called bell bottoms.

flounce. Gathered strip of fabric applied to a skirt, usually at the hem.

gathered skirt. Style made from fabric rectangles and gathered at the waist.

gathering. A method of drawing in fullness by tightening parallel rows of loose stitching.

gaucho pants. Wide-legged pants that reach to mid-calf or the tops of high boots, inspired by South American cowboy garment.

godet. Triangular piece of fabric inserted into a seam to create a flared look.

gore. Skirt panel that is narrow at the waist and widens toward the hem. Gores are stitched together to create fullness, as in a four-gore or six-gore skirt.

grain. Straight threads of a woven fabric, i.e., the lengthwise and crosswise grain.

half-moon pocket. Semicircle pocket commonly seen on Western shirts.

harem pants. Long, full pants gathered into a band at the ankle. Also called Turkish trousers.

hip huggers. Pants that rest below the waist, at hip level, quite popular in the 1960s and 1970s. Also called hipsters.

hobble skirt. Skirt style that is gathered or pleated into the waistband and so sharply tapered in at the calf-length or ankle-length hemline that it hampers walking. Similar to the balloon skirt and tulip skirt.

hot pants. Extremely short, tight shorts popular in the 1970s.

inseam. Inner leg seam of trousers, from crotch point to hem.

inseam pocket. Pocket stitched into the side seam and invisible from the outside.

inverted pleat. Pleat formed from two pleats that face each other and meet along the center of the pleat. See page 52.

Jamaica shorts. Named after Jamaican resort locations, these shorts are shorter than Bermudas, reaching to mid-thigh.

jeans. See blue jeans.

jodhpurs. Riding pants that are loose and billowy from the hips to just below the knees, and then very tight to the ankles.

jumpsuit. One-piece garment adapted from work coveralls that zips or buttons up the front. Also called boilersuit. See page 112.

kangaroo pocket. Large pocket on the center front of a garment.

kangaroo skirt. Maternity style that has a front cut-out or stretch panel to accommodate the growing abdomen.

kick pleat. A short inverted pleat at the hemline of a narrow skirt, usually at center back or the side, that eases movement.

knickers. Loose pants gathered or pleated into a band just below the knees. Also called knickerbockers and plus fours.

knife pleats. Narrow pleats all pressed in the same direction. See page 52.

Lycra.® Stretchy manmade fiber made by E.I. DuPont, commonly used for girdles, swimsuits, sports clothing, and other garments requiring all-over stretch. Some cotton knits and wools have a small amount of Lycra in them, to provide flexibility and memory. Sometimes called Spandex.

maxi skirt. Ankle-length skirt.

micro skirt. Extremely short skirt, reaching just below the seat.

midi skirt. Mid-calf skirt.

miniskirt. Short skirt, ending well above the knee, usually at mid-thigh.

New Look. A post-World War II fashion look created by Christian Dior that was characterized by voluminous skirts, cinched-in waists, and short jackets with sloping shoulders. See page 13.

outseam. Outer leg seam of trousers, from waist to hem.

overalls. Pants with an attached front panel or bib and shoulder straps. Originally worn by farmers, railroad workers, and painters.

painter's pants. Loose pants, usually in white or natural heavyweight cotton, with loops at the side seams for holding paintbrushes.

palazzo pants. Long, wide-legged, flowing pants that look like long culottes, often made in sheer, fluid fabrics.

pants suit. Tailored suit of man-styled pants and jacket.

pareo. Style of wrap skirt, derived from Polynesian dress, formed by wrapping a fabric panel around the body and tying at the waist, shoulder, or neck. Also called sarong. See page 121.

patch pocket. Pocket stitched to the outside of a garment, with or without a flap.

peasant skirt. Full skirt gathered into the waistband, like a dirndl, and often trimmed with bands of embroidery.

pedal pushers. Straight pants, extending to just below the knee, popular during the 1950s.

pegged skirt/trousers. Style that is pleated or gathered at the waist, loose at the hips, and tapered to a narrow width at the hem.

petal skirt. Skirt style with overlapping panels of fabric shaped like the petals of a tulip. Also called tulip skirt.

piping. Folded bias band stitched into a seam for a decorative edging effect. Band can be folded over cords of varying thicknesses for different effects.

pleats. Folds of fabric, usually pressed flat, that draw in fullness and provide garment shaping. See page 52 for a discussion of pleats.

plus fours. See knickers.

pocketing fabric. A tightly woven, durable, smooth-finish cotton fabric, sometimes called Silesia, used for pocket bags.

prairie skirt. Long, full skirt gathered at the waist and worn over a slightly longer, ruffled petticoat or trimmed with a wide hemline ruffle.

rise. Pants measurement from the crotch to the waist.

rolled hem. Method of hemming sheer or delicate fabrics, such as chiffon. The raw edge is rolled between the fingers and hand stitched or sewn with a special machine attachment.

sailor pants. Wide-legged pants, usually bell-bottomed, with a buttoned front panel.

sarong. Style of skirt or dress formed by wrapping a fabric panel around the body and tying at the waist, shoulder, or neck. See pareo.

skorts. Shorts with a front skirt panel.

sloper. Basic fitting or master pattern made to individual measurements.

stay. Any form of reinforcing or stabilizing garment construction. Includes the use of stay tape, seam binding, stay stitching, and the incorporation of a fabric panel to preserve garment shape.

stirrup pants. Slim pants, usually made of a knit fabric, with a strap that fits underneath the instep of the foot, to preserve the tapered silhouette.

stitch in the ditch. Stitching in the "well" or impression of a previously stitched seam. A quick method of joining two layers invisibly.

stovepipes. Tight, narrow-legged pants popular in the 1960s. Also called drainpipes.

Strauss, Levi. Originator of blue jeans or "Levis." See page 36.

straight skirt. Slim skirt style, usually with a few pleats at the waist for shaping and a slit or kick pleat at the hem for ease of movement.

sunray pleats. See accordion pleats.

tiered skirt. Straight skirt with layers of flounces, each one cut a bit larger than the previous one.

toreador pants. Tight pants, extending to just below the knee, popular in the 1950s.

true. Redrawing an altered seamline so it is unbroken and continuous.

true bias. A fabric's 45-degree diagonal direction. See page 28 for a discussion of bias.

trumpet flares. Slim skirt or pants style that flares out sharply at the hem.

tulip skirt. Skirt style that is gathered into the waistband, tapered in at the hemline, and sometimes has overlapping petal-shaped fabric panels.

walking shorts. Shorts that reach almost to the knee. Also called Bermuda shorts.

welt pocket. Tailored pocket style in which the lower edge of the pocket opening is protected by a folded piece of fabric called a welt. The upper edge of the pocket opening often has a flap.

wrap skirt. Skirt style that wraps around the body and buttons or ties at the side.

yoke skirt. Skirt style with a shaped and fitted upper portion, usually extending from the waist to the hip, from which the remaining skirt fabric is draped, pleated, or gathered.

INDEX